Alexander Pennecuik

An Historical Account of the Blue Blanket

craftsmens banner - containing the fundamental principles of the good-town, with the powers and prerogatives of the crafts of Edinburgh. Second Edition

Alexander Pennecuik

An Historical Account of the Blue Blanket
craftsmens banner - containing the fundamental principles of the good-town, with the powers and prerogatives of the crafts of Edinburgh. Second Edition

ISBN/EAN: 9783337369323

Printed in Europe, USA, Canada, Australia, Japan

Cover: Foto ©Andreas Hilbeck / pixelio.de

More available books at **www.hansebooks.com**

AN HISTORICAL ACCOUNT

OF THE

BLUE BLANKET;

OR,

CRAFTSMENS BANNER:

CONTAINING THE

FUNDAMENTAL PRINCIPLES,

OF THE

GOOD-TOWN;

WITH THE

Powers and Prerogatives of the CRAFTS of EDINBURGH, &c.

The SECOND EDITION, Enlarged: And adorned with the Fourteen Incorporations' Arms.

PSAL. lx. 4. *Thou haft given a Banner unto them that fear thee, that it may be difplayed becaufe of the Truth*

EDINBURGH:

Printed by ALEXANDER ROBERTSON.
Sold at his Printing Office, in Niddery's Wynd.
M,DCC,LXXX.

To the READER.

AN introduction, although common, is not very necessary here, as the compiler of the following treatise, with unwearied diligence, searched the ancient records for the Historical account of the Blue Blanket, which is the Craftsmens Banner, containing the fundamental privileges of the good Town; as also, the powers and prerogatives of the Crafts of Edinburgh.

Mr Alexander Pennecuik, who was a burgess and guild brother in the Good Town, searched out records, which had been neglected by all other historians who had pretended to give authentic accounts of Edinburgh, &c. Upon the 7th of April, 1722, he gave in his manuscript of the Blue Blanket to the Convener of the Fourteen Incorporations, in order that they might judge of its authenticity, which, being very narrowly inspected by proper antiquarians, was found just, and the Fourteen Incorporations appointed two of their Craftsmen, to give a public testimony of their approbations; which they did, in a letter, recorded before the preface.

In this Edition the publisher has taken care not to vary from the old original language of the charters belonging to the Crafts of Edinburgh, and likewise annexed the Set or Charter for the government of the City of Edinburgh, which clearly points out, both to the Magistrates and the Fourteen Incorporations, their powers of electing and being elected.

As also, the Coats of Arms for each of the Fourteen Incorporations, with their dates when granted, &c.

May the *Worshipful the* Deacons of Crafts, *and all the members of the* Fourteen Incorporations *in the* Good Town of Edinburgh, *live in unity and love; and, in the worst of times, support and maintain the honours and freedom of the* Blue Blanket, *till the last trump rend the ætherial sky, is the ardent prayer of,*

Worthy fellow-citizens,

Your devoted humble servant,

The PUBLISHER.

To the Worshipful

The DEACONS of CRAFTS,

And the remanent Members of the

Fourteen Incorporations in the Good Town of *Edinburgh*.

I PRESENT you with an abridgment of the glorious actions of your predecessors; who, by a dutiful attachment to their Sovereign, suffering by impious rebels, shewed their hearts enflam-

The Epistle Dedicatory.

ed with loyalty, their hands were thunder, and their deeds miracles. You enjoy the honours and privileges which they procured from the Monarchs of SCOTLAND, as rewards for their heroic atchievements. You are, what the greatest Princes and warriors in Europe, triumphant in the field of battle, and pressed down to the grave with laurels, have aspired to Knights of the HOLY GHOST; your BANNER being called in original writs, *The Banner of the Holy Ghost.* Study then to imitate your worthy ancestors in their illustrious virtues, and inviolably maintain the privileges of your *MAGNA CHARTA*: It is a sacred depositum, which you are bound in conscience, as well as through interest, to defend. If your enemies should dare to invade your prerogatives, granted by Kings, the

The Epistle Dedicatory.

fountains of law and honour, let the nation's motto be yours:

Nemo me impune lacesset.

REMEMBER King David's saying, which is very snug to the purpose, Psalm lx. 4. *He hath given a banner unto them that fear him; that it may be displayed because of the truth,* Selah.

I HAVE, with unweared pains, collected the materials of the ensuing history, from original authentic manuscripts, and historians of unquestionable veracity; and I humbly dedicate it to you the CRAFTS of EDINBURGH; wishing prosperity to YOU and the GOOD TOWN, whose pillars and chief corner-stones you have always proved. May the Psalmist's prayer for Zion be granted unto her, *Peace be within her walls,*

The Epistle Dedicatory.

and prosperity within her palaces: May they prosper that love her, and seek her peace continually. May the inimitable poet's lines become a fulfilled prophecy, to be applied to our SOVEREIGN CITY:

Now, like a maiden Queen, she will behold
From her high turrets hourly suitors come:
The East *with incense, and the* West *with gold,*
Will stand like supplients to receive her doom.
The silver Forth, *her own domestic flood,*
Shall bear her vessels, like a sweeping train,
And often wish, as of her mistress proud,
With longing eyes to meet her face again.
The vent'rous merchant who design'd more far,
And touches on our hospitable shore,

The Epistle Dedicatory.

Chaim'd with the splendor of this Northern Star,
Shall here unload him, and depart no
   more.

DRYD. Ann. Mirr.

THAT this may happen, and your INCORPORATIONS may flourish with blessings of the *Upper and the Nether Springs*, is the earnest prayer of,

Worthy Fellow-Citizens,

Your devoted humble servant,

Edinburgh,
August 1. 1722.

ALEXANDER PENNECUIK.

Copy of an Epistle from two CRAFTS-
MEN *in* Edinburgh *to the* Author.

"SIR,

"SINCE you have put an high
" respect upon us, to commu-
" nicate in manuscript your histori-
" cal account of the *Blue Blanket,* and
" to ask our advice about its publica-
" tion; having carefully and with
" pleasure perused it, we return you
" our sincere thanks for your elabo-
" rate enquiry into the concealed
" honours of the trades: But being
" diffident of our sufficiency to
" judge of an historian, we laid it
" before the ablest of our brethren,
" who earnestly sollicite you may

" send it abroad. You have troden
" in unbeaten paths, the subject hav-
" ing been over-looked by all Scottish
" historians. As we question not
" but you will oblige the world by
" publishing the honours of the
" BLANKET, so assure yourself of
" a tribute of praise from all *Crafts-*
" *men,* especially from,

" S I R,

" Your humble servants,

G. H.

Edinburgh,
1st *September,* 1722.

W. D."

A General Preface.

Touching CRAFTSMEN, and the Honorary Offices they have enjoyed in Church and State.

WHEN the Omnipotent Architect had built the glorious fabrick of this world; upon a review of his works, he pronounced, they were all very good, and rested from his labours: The Almighty could have spoke the world into being in a moment; but out of the depth of infinite wisdom, spent six days in its creation, that man might learn still to be usefully employed, copying after the example of his Lord and Lawgiver. Though his deputy Adam was the first and greatest of monarchs, whose dominions extended from pole to pole, in a state of innocence, before sin had blasted the beauty of Eden, and nature spontaneously yielded her fruits; yet was he not to eat the bread of idleness, having his task daily assigned him, as is inimitably expressed by the matchless Milton, in his beautiful descripion of Adam awaking his charming Eve.

Awake, the morning shines, and the fresh field
Calls us ; we lose the prime, to mark how spring
Our tended plants, how blows the Citron groves :
What drops the myrrh, and what the balmy reed,
How nature paints her colours, how the bee
Sits on the bloom, extracting liquid sweets.

His eldest son, by right of primogeniture, fiar of a fair inheritance, was educate a plowman, and his brother a grazier. The fall of man introduced those liberal sciences, divinity, law and physick; but though we had continued pure, as when we dropt from the fingers of our Maker, mechanic arts had been necessary. In the infancy of the world, before the wrangling of lawyers, the sophistry of philosophers, and turbulent factions of divines had debauched mankind, artists were in the highest repute. Adah bare Jabal, the father of all such as dwell in tents, and his brother's name was Jubal, the father of all such as handle the harp and organ, *Gen.* iv. 20. and *verse* 22. Tubal Cain was an instructer of every artificer in brass and iron.

It is much to the honour of Craftsmen, that holy Joseph, husband to the blessed Virgin Mary, mother of the Son of GOD, was a carpenter, though it leſſened our Lord's eſteem amongſt the populace, who tauntingly cried (Matth. xiii. 35.) *Is not this the carpenter's ſon?* And if we credit the earlieſt eccleſiaſtic hiſtorians, the glorious Redeemer of mankind, before his public entrance upon the miniſterial office, laboured with his hands in the ſhop: Though he called St. Matth. from the cuſtoms, to evidence the extent and conquering power of his grace; yet the moſt of his apoſtles and diſciples, who ſpread the everlaſting goſpel, and ſupplanted the government of Satan, purchaſed food with the ſweat of their brows.

God ſeems to have put a diſtinguiſhing honour upon tradeſmen, that in all ages, men of the greateſt learning, and the nobleſt heroes, have ſprung from their loins; Porus, monarch of the Indies, was the ſon of a barber, and wrought himſelf as a tinker. Braydillus, prince of the Sclavonians, ſon of a collier. Artagorus, Governor of the Cyconians, ſon of a cook. Agathocles, King of Sicily, ſon of a potter. The good Archbiſhop Villageſius, ſon of a carter; for which reaſon he took wheels for his armorial-bearing. Cardinal Woolſey, Chancellor of England, was begot by a butcher. One of the greateſt ſtateſmen of any age, Cardinal Julius Alberoni, by a gardener: And our famous countryman Mr. Law, by a goldsmith of Edinburgh.

As the seed of mechanics have risen to the highest dignities, so mechanics themselves have swayed sceptres, proven the bravest generals, the wisest statesmen, and the greatest monarchs; tho' the unthinking mass of mankind may despise a person for low birth · The first circumstance of life ought to have no influence in our judgment of a great man; because we cannot pretend to be the children of whom we please; and that a man may owe his birth to a prince, whose natural temper and inclinations discover more meanness of birth than if he were the son of a weaver: whereas nothing is more glorious than, when notwithstanding of the defect of education, a man knows how to rectify and elevate the inclinations which an obscure birth naturally inclines to be servile.

Quintus Cincinnatus, when called to the Government of Rome, was found hard at Plow; being saluted by the name of Dictator, invested with purple, honoured with the faces, and other ensigns of magistracy, was desired to take journey; after a little pause, he answered with tears in his eyes, *Then, for this year, my poor farm must be unsown.* Taking leave of his family, he performed his office with that prudence and justice, that he proved the admiration of the world: And having finished his dictatorship, returned again to his plow. Arsaces, from being a private mechanic, was called to found the Parthian empire: and such an one was Tamberlane, the vanquisher of Asia. Peter du Brosse Chirurgeon, was high chamberlain of France, and secretary to King Philip III. Massianello, a Neapolitan fisherman, raised an army of 50000, 7th of July, 1647, and trampled on the government of Naples, till they were obliged to yield to the demands of the people groaning under the burthen of exorbitant taxes. The Anabaptists in Munster, chused John of Leyden, a taylor, for their King, A. D. 1535. Zeno, the famous bishop of Constantia, was a weaver, who lived till he was past an hundred years of age; and though he was the most eminent bishop, and had the largest diocese in that country, kept a weaver's shop, and wrought himself daily at the loom to clothe the naked. When the peasants of Upper Austria rose up against P. Maximilian, Elector of Bavaria, A. D. 1627, their army consisted of 60,000; it was commanded by Stephen Tudiner, a hatter; and after his death by Walmer, a shoemaker, killed by Count Papenheim. And I cannot omit to hint at the beautiful story of Mr. Edmond, a Baxter, and son of a baxter in Stirling, who shewed such unparalleled valour in the Swedish wars, under the command of that immortal thunderbolt of war, Gustavus

vi   *A General Preface.*

Adolphus, that he became a general; his swimming the Danube, and, by an artful stratagem, carrying off the General of the Imperialists, and other marvellous actions of his life, are recorded in the chronicles of Sweden. In his old age he returned to his native country, Scotland, and built a stately manse at Stirling, which he doned to the Church.

HISTORIANS, ancient and modern, not only record the martial atchievements, but the singular sanctity of mechanics, not to mention the faith of a shoemaker, under the reign of a King of Persia, who removed a mountain by a holy harangue, related by Paulus Venetus de Rebus Orientalibus, and Nazianzen Causen, in his holy court, as favouring too much of a morkish fable; nor the known story of Crispianus, who suffered by the cruelty of Maximilian. The Church records a noble army of martys, who died for the Protestant faith in the reign of Henry VIII. and Mary, Sovereigns of England.

  John Mace, surgeon
  Richard Ferus, goldsmith
  Mr. Gilles, cutler
  Robert Hackets Arthur ⎫
  Thomas Bond   ⎪
  John Hart   ⎬ shoemakers
  John Curd   ⎪
  John Hoys   ⎭

John Cooksbury } tanners
John Hammond
John Bennet
Andrew Heuet } taylors
John Warner
William Corberley
George Eagles, minister
William Picket } butchers
Thomas Cob
Stephen Knight, barber
George Tankerfield, cook
Thomas Hudson, glover
Thomas Thomkins
William Bamford
Nicolas Chamberland
John Cavell } weavers
John Spence
Richard Nicolas
John Careless
John Leaf, candlemaker
Nicolas Hall } masons
John Spicers
John Tudson } smiths
John Went
John Clement
Thomas Avington } joiners
Thomas Harland
Thomas Ravendell, currier.

Sanctitatis radiis, in orbe refulsit.

Behold the martyrs who for truth have dy'd,
Heaven's glory now, and Britain's greatest pride.

No Popiſh flames to them a period give,
Their memoirs eternally ſhall live.

WISE Princes and States have always had mechanics in higheſt eſtimation. The Grand Seignior, though one of the greateſt Princes in Europe, is always educate in ſome handy craft. The Dutch, and the Czar of Muſcovy, by encouraging Craftſmen, have made their countries flouriſh, and are become the terror and envy of their neighbours. King Charles II. was an excellent worker in ivory: neither the affairs of ſtate, nor pleaſures of his court, could divert him from his taſk at the Turner's loom. Lewis the XIV. of France, was ſo exquiſitely good at making of watches, that he was equalled by few in his reign.

WHAT reſpect the Kings of Scotland have put upon tradeſmen, the following hiſtory of the *Blue Blanket*, or, *Craftſmens Banner*, will declare. They have had the happineſs to taſte the bounty of our Princes in the higheſt honours: For this order of the *Blanket*, originally of eccleſiaſtic inſtitution, is confirmed by the royal ſanction. It had its riſe about the 1200 year of GOD, when the Croiſade was carried on by Pope Urban the Second; and ſo is older than any of the orders of knighthood in Europe, ſave that of St. Andrew, or the Thiſtle, which had its original about the 800, when the King of Scots and Picts made war againſt Athelſton King of the Weſt Saxons; and that of the Star, or bleſſed Virgin, which, as Selden, in his titles of honour, remarks, had its riſe in the year 1022: for that order of St. George, or the Garter, was not inſtitute till the year 1345, that of St. Michael, not till 1448, and that of the Golden Fleece 1429. So that I may ſay the words of Doctor Helen in his preface to his Hiſtory of the Engliſh nobility, *Kings have ſo much of God in them, whoſe deputies they are on earth, as many times, where they find merit and deſert, they raiſe the poor out of the duſt, that they may ſet them with Princes, even the Princes of the people.*

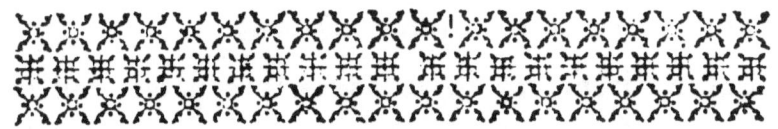

AN

HISTORICAL ACCOUNT

OF THE

BLUE BLANKET;

OR,

CRAFTSMENS BANNER.

CONTAINING

The fundamental Principles of the Government of the Good Town, Powers, and Prerogatives of the CRAFTS of EDINBRGH.

THE metropolitan city of Scotland, by some historians, (as Buchanan observes) either through ignorance or ill-will, called Valla Dolorosa, the Doleful Valley; by the Pictish records, Castrum Puellarum, the Maiden

Castle, from its royal and impregnable castle, built by Cruthenus Camelon, King of the Picts, where the daughters of the Pictish Kings were kept working at their needles, till married; which, for strength, and command of prospect, may challenge precedency of the best in Britain. Some of the ancient Scotts called it Castrum Allatum, others, Dunedinum; and the latter Edinum, which we render *Edinburgh;* it is situated on the declining of an hill, from whence she views her tributary river Forth, encompassed about with fertile fields, spacious pastures, and goodly gardens, grown by degrees, in such magnificence of buildings, as to stand in competition, almost, with any in Europe; and justly merits the encomium Dr. Arthur Johnston bestowed upon her:

That Edinburgh *may view the heavens at will,*
'Tis built upon a lofty rising hill.
The fields and rivers, which her hand-maids be,
She thence views, and the tributary sea:
And when the sun displays his morning light,
The palace doth present itself to sight.
That princely dwelling under Arthur Seat,
Adorn'd by most ingenius art of late;
Towards the west the glorious castle stands;
Which with its thunder giveth loud commands.
Each citizen hath such a house, that it
May Peers of greatest quality well fit.

The threats of foes do not make them dismay'd,
Nor need they be by their assaults afraid.
Sure, for a Kingly city, none can wish
A seat that's more convenient than this.

It is not only beautiful, but ancient, though the time when it was founded is not easily discovered. The magistrates of Edinburgh, in their congratulatory harangue to King James the VI. of Scotland, and I. of England, recorded in the *Muses Welcome to that Prince*, assert, it was builded by Fergusius, the first builder of this kingdom, three hundred and thirty years before the Incarnation of Christ.

In our fierce and frequent wars with the Picts, Danes, Romans and English, this city was so often destroyed, her monuments and charters lost, that her original cannot be well documented. The first Charter I find in her favours is granted by King Alexander I. firnamed *the Good*, and the second by his successor St. David. It is generally agreed upon, that it was made a Burgh Royal by King William I. in whose reign a fervour of devotion, encouraged by Pope Urban II. seized the spirits of the princes and cavaliers of Europe, under the command of Godfrey of Bulloign, to rescue Palestine, and the city of Jerusalem out of the hands of Saladine, and to pluck the sepulchre of Jesus from the possession of Infidels. The zealous Pontiff was afflicted that the Holy Land, the city of God, the inheritance of Jesus, should be sullied by Infidels, Saracens and Turks; who, in some measure, might be said to have driven our Lord from his capital, that the cross, the glory and ornament of crowned heads, should be trampled upon by the vilest of Adam's posterity. Therefore he inculcated the necessity of taking arms, and united all the powers of Chistendom; and to whet their courage, promised to those that would join in this holy service, a plenary indulgence, that is, a remission of all penances imposed by confessors.

Vast numbers of Scots mechanics having followed this holy war, taking with them a *Banner*, bearing this inscription out of the li. Psalm, *In bona vo untate tua edificenter muri Jerusalem.* Upon their returning home, and glorying that they were amongst the fortunate who placed the Christian standard of the cross in the place that Jesus Christ had consecrated with his blood, they dedicated this *Banner*, which they stiled *The Banner of the Holy Ghost*, to St. Eloi's altar in St. Giles's church in Edinburgh; which, from its colour, was called *The Blue Blanket*.

Though none of our historians mention the original institution of the *Blue Blanket*, nor is there any vouchers for it, saving old imperfect manuscripts; yet, it is highly probable, it had its rise from the Croisade, or Holy War: for Monsieur Cheverau in his History of the World, tells us that Scotland was engaged in that war, and sold or mortgaged their estates for that expedition; and that she was amongst the forward nations in it. Pere Maimbourg, Histoir des Croisades, informs us, that the knights of St. Lazarus, an order of men educate to the holy war, were numerous every where, but especially in Scotland and France; as appears by the charters and grants of princes in their favours; and the distinctive crosses they wore, evince, that the Scots were as forward, gallant, and zealous in the service, as any of their neighbours.

Our histories bear, that a great many of the Scots went to that war, under the command of Allan, Lord great Steward of Scotland; and they, with their confederates, got possession of Jerusalem in 1099.

When Saladine prevailed against the Christian arms, William, King of Scotland, assisted the war with money, and sent supplies of men to the meritorious action, under the command of David his brother, and that five thousand Scots had their share in the Mallheurs and successes of that unfortunate enterprize. And if we may believe Boethius in Vita Gull. the renowned city Ptolemais was taken by the good conduct of Earl David, brother to the King of Scots, Anno 1091, and that the Christian intelligencer was one Oliver, a Scotsman.

THIS *Blue Blanket*, whose original I have endeavoured to discover, was, in the dark times of Popery, held in such religious veneration, that whenever mechanics were artfully wrought upon by the clergy, to display their holy colours, it served for many uses, and they never failed of success in their attempts; which is not to be wondered at: For as the learned and judicious Doctor Abercromby observes in the Life of St. David, King of Scotland, speaking of the battle of the Standard, ' So good a use have churchmen in
' all ages known to make of religious pageantries,
' and so much have the vulgar been misled into the
' belief of heavenly protection, by the Legerde-
' main tricks of spiritual guides, who, while they
' have no other view but to gratify their private
' passions, muster the deluded people into rebel-
' lion.

HAVING thus accounted for the original of the order of the *Blue Blanket*, I may fairly infer, that it is as ancient, and more honourable than the

English order of the Garter, the institution whereof, some ascribe to a garter falling occasionally from the Countess of Salisbury; though others affirm, the Garter was given in testimony of that bond of love whereof the knights and fellows of it were to be tied to one another, and all of them to the King. And others make it still more ancient, giving it the same original with the Blue Blanket, relating, that when King Richard I. of England was at war against the Turks and Saracens in the Holy Land, the tediousness whereof began to discourage his soldiers, he, to quicken their courage, tied about the legs of several choice knights a garter, or small thong of leather, the only stuff he had at hand, that as the Romans used to bestow crowns and garlands for encouragement, so this might provoke them to stand together, and fight valiantly for their king.

The Crafts of Edinburgh, having this order of the *Blanket* to glory in, may justly take upon them the title of *Knights of the Blanket*, or, *Chevaliers of arms:* For, as the learned Skene, *De Verborum Significatione*, in his title, *Banrents* observes, that Banrents are called *Chevaliers of Arms*, or *Knights*, who, obtaining great honours and dignities, have power and privileges granted to them by the King, to raise and lift up a banner, with a company of men of weir, either horse or foot; which cannot be done by any save baronets, without the King's special licence, as Pasquiers, lib. 2. *Desrecherchères de la France*, ch. 9. fol. 100. by sundry arguments proves, and Dr. Smith, in his Treatise of the Commonwealth of England, lib. 1. chap. 17. informs us, that Knights Banrents are allowed to display their arms on a banner in the King's host.

As the Knights of St. George have their meeting at Windsor castle, and these of the Thistle in the royal palace of Holyrood-house, so the Knights of the *Blanket* have theirs at St. Eloi, who was a French bishop and their guardian, his altar, to which they mortify considerable sums for the maintenance of a chaplain, and reparation of the ornaments of the chapel ; as appears from the Craftsmens seal of cause, the tenor of which runs thus :

Seal of Cause for the Hammermen of Edinburgh.

' TILL all and syndry quham it effiers,
' quhais knawledge thir present letters shall to cum,
' Andrew Bartrem Provost of Edinburgh, George
' Edwardson, John of Livington, Alexander
' Crawford, James Aikman, and John Bisset,

' baillziefs of the said burgh, greeting; for sae
' meikle as, the hedifmen and maifters of the
' hamerman, and maifters of the hammerman-
' craft, baith black-fmythes, gold-fmythes, lori-
' mers, fadlars, cutlars, bucklar-makers, armour-
' ars, peudrars, and all uthers within the said
' burgh, has humyly menyt and fhawin, baith to
' our Soveraine Lord the King, and to us, the
' the great fkaith, lak and dangire done to thaim,
' and the great dampnage, hurt and prejudife
' done to our Soveraine Lord's realme and lieges
' in thir points that efter folows, throw the
' quhilks the faids Craftfmen are heryit and put to
' povertie, befekand our Lord's gud grace, and
' us in his name, of remed and reformacioune
' thairof, and to fett fic ftatuts and ways thairup-
' on that the faids dampnages, lak and dangirs may
' be ifcewit, and the said craft of hamyrmen ex-
' ercit in time cumying, to the honour of our
' Soverane Lord and his realme, and to the wele
' and profit of the faids Craftifmen, and all uthers
' his lieges; that is to fay in the firft, that the
' faid Craft is abufit, and the maifters and hedif-
' men theirof gretly fkaithit by the daily markat
' maid in Cremys, and be vile perfons throw the
' hie ftreet, and on the bak half of the town, in
' bachlying of the hammyrmenis work and thair
' craft in lak and difhonouring of our said burgh,

' and in breking of the gud rule, lovable and old
' statuts, maid diverse tymes thairupon of before:
' We herefor understanding the reasonable suppli-
' cacioune, and just petitioune of the said Craf-
' tismen, desyring to sett remed, and doe justice
' thairuntill, to the honour of the said burgh, and
' commone wele of the said Craftismen and this
' hale realme, has, according to our Soverane
' Lord writinis and charges gevan to us thairup-
' on, the common profit byng always considerit,
' statut, devist and ordain, and be thir our present
' letters statuts, devisis and ordainis, that in time
' cumyng, thair be na opyn market maid, or usit
' be quhatsumevir personis, of any wark perteny-
' ing to the said hammyrmen of thair craft, in
' schewing theirof in hands upone the hie streeit,
' nor in the Cremys, nay in Burds, nor utherways
' within the said burgh, nor in thir buthis, ex-
' cept alanarly the markat day. *Item,* That na
' personis of the hammyrman craft sett up buth
' to wyrk within the said burgh quhill he be maid
' an freeman thairof, and be examinit be thrie of
' the best maisters of the said craft, gif he be
' sufficient, and wyrkand goood and sovir wark,
' fyne stuff, and habill to serve our Soverane Lord
' and his lieges, and then to be admittit to sett
' up buth, he payant therefor to the said uphald
' of divyne so be done at St. Eloi's altar, and re-
' paracioune of the ornaments thairof fourtey

' shillings. *Item*, That every Craftsman that
' taks ane prentise to tech him the said craft with-
' in the said burgh, sal pay for his entry to the up-
' hald of the said altar, and the ornaments thair-
' of, twenty shillings. *Item*. That non of the
' saids craftsmen tak any uther seit man to wyrk
' on the said craft quhill his prentischip be fulfil-
' lit and completit under the pain of twenety
' shillings, *Item*. that nane of the saids Craftis-
' men ressave nor lat wark within his buthe ony
' man, without he be uther his prentise or seit
' servand, sa that the maister of the buthe sal an-
' suer for his wark and fynenes thairof. *Item*,
' That nane of the said craftsmen resett, tak, nor
' fee an uther manis prentis or servand, nor give
' him wark, without it be clearly understaund
' that he be free of uther menis servis. *Item*,
' Upon ilk Saturday afternoon, that twa or thrie
' of the worthyest maisters and of maist knaw-
' lage of the said craft, chosine thairto be the haill
' fallowship, pass with thair officiar, and serch
' and se all menys wark in the said craft, gif it be
' sufficient in stuff and warkmanship, gud and
' habill wark to serve our Soverane Lord's lieges
' with: And quahair it beis fundyn faltive, to
' forbid the samyne, under the pain of escheating
' thairof als aft as he beis fundyne faltive. *Item*,
' That all thir craftsmen above writen sal convene
' tyme and place to be thocht expedyent als aft as

' thay plaife, to common upon the breaking of
' thir ftatuts above expremit, and to certifie the
' prouoft and bailzies thairof that fal be for the
' tyme, that reformacioune and punicion may be
' done thairupon as effiers. *Item*, That every
' man breker of thir forwrittine ftatuts, pay for
' ilk ane of thaim als aft as thay happen to be bro-
' kin in his defalt, aught fhillings to be taken but
' favore, to the reparacioune of the faid altar
' and ornamentis thairof, and that all men of the
' faid craft doe and fulfil her ald ufand confuetud
' in all thyngs to the uphald of divyne fervace at
' the faid altar oukly and dayly, and ane honour-
' abill chaplin thairof to thair craft as effiers;
' and gif the maifters and hedifmen of the faid
' craft dois nocht thair dilligence, to caufe all
' thir ftatuts above writtine to be obfervit and
' kepit, ans faits thairof to be ferchit and punyfht,
' that thay fall be correct and punyfht thairfor
' be the proveft and baillzies, as fall be fene con-
' fonant to reafone. And this to all quham it ef-
' fiers, or may effier, we mak knawn faytfullie be
' thir our prefent lettirs, and in witneffing thair-
' of we have, at the command of our Soverane
' Lord, and defyre and requeft of the fayds Craf-
' tifmen, maid our common fele of caufe to be
' hyngin to thir prefents, at Edinburgh the 12th
' day of April, the zier of God a thoufand and
' four hundred ninety and fix ziers.

Ratification in Favours of the Hammermen of Edinburgh.

'ATT Edinburgh the fixt day of September
' 1681 years, our Soveraign Lord, with advice
' and confent of his eftats of parliament prefent-
' ly conveened by his Majefties fpeciall authority,
' hes ratifyed and approven, and hereby ratifies
' and approves the haill rights, privileges, immu-
' nities and caufualties, granted to, and in favores
' of the deacon, boxmafters, mafters, patrons,
' and remanent members of the Magdalane cha-
' ple, confifting of fmiths, cutlers, faidlers, lori-
' mers, armorers, peuthereis, fhear-fmiths, and
' all others incorporat, or to be incorporate with
' them, by our Soveraigne Lord, or any on
' other of his Majefties royall predeceffors, or by
' the provoft, bailhes, and Toun Council of the
' faid burgh of Edinburgh, and mortifiecations
' granted to them, by whatfomever perfon or per-
' fons, of whatfomever date, tenor, or contents
' the famin be of, and bear ; and particularly,
' but prejudice of the faid generality, an feal of
' caufe granted to them by the magiftrats and
' common Council of the faid burgh of Edin-
' burgh, upon the twelvth day of April, 1496,
' as the famin in itfelf more fully bears, in the
' haill heads, claufes, and articles therein con-

' tained, after the form and tenor thereof, in all
' points, and wills, and grants, and for his Ma-
' jesty, and his Highness successors, with advice
' and consent foresaid, decerns, declares, and or-
' dains this present general confirmation to be als
' sufficient, valid and effectual in all respects, as if
' the saids haill rights, grants and privileges;
' and particularly but prejudice of the foresaid ge-
' nerality, the seall of cause, and gifts of morti-
' fication above mentioned, were *de verbo in ver-*
' *bum* herein expressly sett doun, ingrossed and
' repeated. Likeas, his Majesty, with advice and
' consent forsaid, hes ratifyed, and hereby ratifies,
' approves, and confirms to the said incorporation
' of hammermen, all and sundry their rights and
' privileges, whereof they have been in use and
' possession; and particularly, of seising and ap-
' prehending of all and whatsomever work belong-
' ing to, or that can be made, furnished and com-
' pleated by them, that shall happen to be import-
' ed within the said burgh, any time hereafter,
' (except upon the mercat day) and there escheat
' and confiscating the one half thereof to his Ma-
' jesties use, and the other half of the samen to the
' use of the poor of the said incorporation. And
' further, discharges and inhibits all, and what-
' somever work belonging to, or can be made,
' furnished and compleated by them, to be in-
' brought, sold, vented or retailed within the said

'burgh, by any perſon or perſons, except within
'the boothes and ſhops of the freemen of the
'ſaid incorporation, but what ſhall happen to be
'inbrought on the mercat day, and vented, ſold,
'and ratiled on the mercat day, at the ordinary
'mercat place, between ten hours in the morning
'and two in the afternoon, and that under the
'pain of confiſcation thereof to the uſes foreſaid:
'Extracted forth of the records of Parliament,
'by me Sir Tho. Murray of Glendoick, Knight
'and Baronet, clerk to his Majeſty's council, re-
'giſter and rols.

'Tho. Murray, *Clerk Regiſter.*'

The trades being thus confirmed in their privileges by the royal ſanction, gave ſuch extraordinary proofs of loyalty, that they eſtabliſhed themſelves in the grace and favour of their Princes; and their loyal actions I ſhall trace, beginning with the reign of

King Robert Bruce.

For many eminent ſervices performed by the crafts, and other citizens of Edinburgh, contained in an charter granted by the ſaid King Robert, dated at Cardroſs, in the 24th year of his reign: He diſpones to the Provoſt, baillies, council, and communities of the ſaid burgh, and their ſucceſfors, the haven of Leith, mills, and other pertinents thereof, to be holden of his Majesty, and succeffors, als freely, and with the fame liberties and commodities, as the fame were enjoyed in the time of King Alexander his predeceffor, of happy memory, for payment of 52 merks. Nor was Edinburgh, by her loyal deportment, lefs in favour with his fucceffor,

King ROBERT the II.

In the beginning of his reign, Edinburgh, to fpeak properly, was not the capital city of Scotland, being only a fmall burgh (which made Walfinghame, and other hiftorians of thefe times, call it a village) the houfes of which, becaufe they were fo often expofed to incurfions from England, being thatched, for the moft part, with ftraw and turf; and then burnt, or demolifhed, were with no great difficulty repaired : for in ancient times, the Highlands was propetly the Scots Kings territories, till the Picts were expelled, who had Edinburgh, and the Lothians in poffeffion, in the reign of King Kenneth II. Anno 839 : But the loyalty of the citizens, impregnable ftrength of the caftle, and the conveniency of the abbey of Holyroodhoufe, in the royal chapel whereof his corpfe is interred, invited the King to dwell, and hold his parliament there. From this proceeded a great concourse of people, who were of course obliged to resort to it, and occasioned these magnificent, but too costly structures, with which it is since crowded. But the loyalty of this city of Edinburgh, was more remarkable In the reign of

King James III.

who having offended his nobles, for advancing Robert Cochran, a mason, to the dignity of secretary of State, and creating him Earl of Mar, James Hommel, a taylor, and one Leonard, a smith, to extraordinary favour, and places of trust, so incensed the ancient Peerage, for enobling these mushrooms, sprung from the dreg of the people, quarrelling the King's arbitrary power, in dispensing these honours, and marshalling those persons whom he had advanced to these high dignities, that in an impetus of passion, they hanged Cochran Earl of Mar over the bridge of Lauder, and raised such violent emotions in the state, that his Majesty, for security of his royal person, was forced to shelter himself in Edinburgh castle. During his confinement there, the English, with whom he was at war, having marched to Edinburgh; and there being a treaty betwixt the Scots and them, of the 2d August 1482; the next day after this cessation, Alexander, Duke of Albany, the King's brother, importuned by the prayers and tears of the Queen, for the King's liberty, by the affiftance of William Bartrem, provoft of Edinburgh *, and with him the whole community, and incorporations of Craftfmen, intirely loving their King, and devoted to his fervice, loyally, and generoufly obliged themfelves to repay to the King the fums of money deburfed by him in view of the marriage betwixt the Duke of Rothfay and his daughter the Lady Cecil: or, if the King did yet incline that the marriage fhould be compleated, they undertook for their Sovereign Lord the King of Scotland, that he fhould concur, conform to his former obligation, providing that their faid Sovereign Lord, or the Lords of his council, or the faids provoft and burghers were informed of the King of England's pleafure and election upon the matter, by the firft of *All Saints* next to come. And the faids citizens furprized and ftormed the caftle of Edinburgh; and to the great diffatisfation of the rebellious nobles, fet their Sovereign at liberty. Thefe furprifing inftances of loyalty and valour, for which they fhall be had in everlafting remembrance, procured from the King a grant of many new privileges, contained in a patent, which they call their *Golden Charter*, dated 1482; particularly, the magiftrates

---

* *Fœd. Ang. Tom.* 12. P. 161. Godfcraft's Hiftory of the *Douglaffes.* *Abercromby*'s Martial Atchivements, *Hawthernden*'s Hiftory.

are made heritable sheriffs within the said burgh, and liberties of the same. And another charter from their said Sovereign Lord, in favours of the said provost, baillies, council and communities of the said burgh, and their successors for ever, of all the customs of the haven of Leith, and road of the same, dated 16th November, 1482, and a confirmation of a charter and infeoffment granted by Sir Robert Logan of Restalrig, to them, of all the passages and ways leading to the haven and harbour of Leith, and from the same; containing divers liberties and immunities.

Indeed they very well deserved the favours bestowed on them; for it is certain, that upon the King of England's sending his servant the Garter King at arms, to let them know, that for several great causes and considerations, he had entirely refused to comply with the marriage betwixt the Duke of Rothsay and his daughter; they repaid all the money, amounting to 6000 merks, which he debursed on that account.

Having traced the *Blue Blanket* to the origen of the Croisade, from whence it undoubtedly had its rise, I cannot pass over in silence the honour put upon it by this monarch, who was the first that gave it the civil sanction, not thinking the above donatives a sufficient reward to the loyal crafts, confirmed to them all the privileges of the *Blue Blanket*, which they claimed by prescription, or an immemorial possession, and ordained it to be called in all time coming, *The standard of the crafts within burgh:* For that King, full of the spirit that warms the blood of absolute monarchs, highly resented the treatment Robert Cochran, mason, by him created Earl of Mar, had met with by his factious nobles, would needs confer this dignity upon the trades, in whom he placed his special confidence. The trades thus honoured, renewed their *banner*; or, to speak in the language of heralds, their *ensign*, by way of Pennon, and the Queen, with her own hands, painted upon it a Saltire, or St. Andrew's Cross, a Thistle, an Imperial Crown, and an Hammer, with the following inscription :

Fear God, and honour the King,
With a long life and prosperous reign,
And we the trades shall ever pray.

THE crafts having now not only the cross, but the crown on their ensign, were as firmly persuaded of success in all their public actings, as Constantine the Great, the first Christian Emperor, in the year 306, of defeating the tyrant Maxentius, when at noon-day he saw a luminous cross in the air, with these words in Greek,

In hoc Signo vinces.

The old nobility and gentry were exceedingly nettled at the proceedings of the King, to re-establish his authority; but in the judgment of wise and loyal men, very unjustly; for, the foundation of all obedience to superiors, are rewards and punishments, and royalty is an invention of Divine Wisdom, for the happiness of subjects; and Kings, being common fathers to their people, are to reward virtue wherever they find it; it is their duty to do it, and the promise of the King of Kings, that they shall do it: *He will take their daughters, and make hem apothecaries, cooks and bakers; and he will take their sons, and appoint them to his chariots, and to be his horsemen, and he will make them captains over thousands. As the wrath of a King is like the roaring of a lion, so in the light of his countenance is life, and his favour as the latter rain.*

As the crafts of Edinburgh, in the reign of his successors, made a very grateful and prudent use of the *Blue Blanket*, with respect to government, so they never failed, with this standard, to chaſtiſe all, who in the leaſt infringed their rights and privileges, which King James VI. takes notice of in his *Baſilicon Dɔron*, or, Advice to his Son and apparent ſucceſſor Henry Prince of Wales, page 164. *The craftſmen think we ſhould be content with their work, how bad ſoever it be ; and if in any thing they be controled, up goes the* Blue Blanket.

As they flouriſhed in the favours of their Sovereign King James III. ſo did they in the reign of that courageous and pious Prince his ſucceſſor,

King James IV.

crowned at Edinburgh, 1489; who, for ſingular acts of loyalty performed by the city of Edinburgh, by his charter of confirmation under the Great Seal, to the ſaid provoſt, baillies, council, and communities of the ſaid burgh, ratified and confirmed the two above charters granted by King James III. and charter granted by Sir Robert Logan of Reſtalrig; which charter of confirmation is dated, at Stirling, the 9th day of March, 1510. And, by another charter, diſponed to them the lands and haven of Newhaven, with the haven, ſilver, and all other profits, duties, liberties and immunities pertaining thereto, dated at Stirling the ſaid 9th of March, 1510. Thus far was the city of Edinburgh honoured and privileged in the reign of King James IV. and were no less so during the government of his son and successor,

King James the V.

For during the wars betwixt him and the Earl of Northumberland, John Armstrong, chief of a gang of thieves, was enticed by the King's officers, to have recourse to the King, who had written a letter to him with his royal hand, to attend him at his palace of Holyrood-house: The King hearing a distinct account of the crimes he was guilty of, ordained him to be committed to gaol, and suffer, with his accomplices, according to law. This notorious highwayman, with the assistance of his followers, drew upon the King in his chamber of audience, who was with much difficulty, rescued by the courtiers and their attendants, and continued in their hostilities, designing to have murdered every soul in the royal palace, till it was noised in the city of Edinburgh, that the King was in eminent danger of being cut off by the hands of bloody ruffians: The crafts of the city rose, and slew every one of the assassins. The story is preserved in memory, not so much by our historians, who give but a faint account of it, as a ballad compiled by one of the greatest poets of that age.

There dwelt a man in fair Westmorland,
John Armstrong *men did him call ;*
He h'd neither lands nor rents coming in,
Yet he kept eightscore men in his hall, &c.
The King he wrote an a letter then,
A letter which was large and long ;
He sign'd it with his own hand,
And he promis'd to do him no wrong.
When this letter came John *him till,*
His heart was as blyth as birds on a tree ;
Never was I sent for before any King,
My father, my grandfather, nor none but me, &c.
By the morrow morning at ten of the clock,
Toward Edinburgh gone was he ;
And with him all his eightscore of men,
Good Lord, an it was a goodly sight to see.
When John *came before the King,*
He fell down low upon his knee ;
O pardon, my Sovereign liege, he said,
O pardon my eightscore men and me.
Thou shalt have no pardon thou traitor Strong,
Nae for thy eightscore men and thee ;
For tomorrow morning by ten of the clock,
Both thou and them shall hang on the gallow tree.
Then John *looked over his left shoulder ;*
Good Lord what a grievous look looked he !
Said, I have asked grace at a graceless face,
Why, there is nane for ye nor me.
But John *had a bright sword by his side*

And it was made of metal so free;
That had not the King stept his foot aside,
He had smitten his head from his fair bodie;
Saying, Fight on, my merry men all,
And see that none of you be tane;
For rather than men should say we were hang'd,
Let them report that we were slain.
God wot the trades of Edinburgh rose,
And sore beset poor John round,
That fourscore and ten of John's best men,
Lay gasping all upon the ground, &c.

Having traced the loyal actions of the citizens, especially the crafts of Edinburgh, through the reigns of several Sovereigns, before I proceed to the reign of Queen Mary, I must take notice of the pious donations of an eminent citizen of Edinburgh, Michael Maquhan, and his spouse, in favours of the Hammermen, (who dedicated and consecrated the *Blue Blanket* to St. Eloi's altar, in St. Gile's church) for founding of the Magdalen Chapel, where they now meet, which is contained in the following charter:

'TO all and sundry, to whois knowledge thir
' presents fall come, and be seen, I Jonet Ryne,
' relict, executrix, and only intromissatrix with the
' goods and gear of umquhil Michael M'Quhan,
' burgess of Edinburg, within peace in our Lord,

' makes known by thir presents, That when the
' said Michael was greatly troubled with an heavy
' deseafe, and oppressed with age, zet mindful of
' eternal life, he esteemed it ane good way to
' obtain eternal life, to erect some Christian work,
' for ever to remain and endure, he left seven
' hundered pound, to be employed for the supple-
' ment of the edifice of the Magdalen chapell, and
' to the other edifices for foundation of the chapel,
' and sustentation of seven poor men, who should
' continually there put furth their prayers to God
' Almighty; for there was many others that had
' promised to mortifye some portion of their goods
' for perfeiting and absolveing of the said wark,
' but they failzied, and withdrew from such ane
' holly and religious work, and altogether refused
' thereupon to confer the samen. Quhilk thing I
' taking heavyly, and pondering it in my heart,
' what in such ane deficle business sould be done;
' at last, I thought night and day upon the fulfill-
' ing of my husband's will, and took upon me the
' burden of the haill wark, and added two thou-
' sand pound to the 700 *l.* left be my husband:
' And I did put furth these soumes wholly, after
' his death, upon the edification of that chapel,
' ornaments thereof, and building of the edifice
' for the habitation of the chaplane, and seven
' poor men, and for buying of land, as well field
' land, as burgh land, and yearly annualrents, for

' the nourishment, sustentation, and clothing of
' them, as hereafter mair largely set down *There-*
' *fore wit ye me*, To the praise and honour of Al-
' mighty God, and of his mother the blissed Vir-
' gine Mary, and of Mary Magdallen, and of the
' haill celestial court, to have erected and edified
' ane certain chapell and hospital house, lyeing in
' the burgh of Edinburgh, upon the south side of
' the King's high street, called the Cowgate, for
' habitation of the foresaid chaplain and poor, and
' that from the foundation thereof; and has dedi-
' cate the samen to the name of Mary Magdallen,
' and has foundit the said chaplain, and seven
' poor, for to give furth their continual prayers un-
' to God for the salvation of the soul of our most
' illustrious Mary Queen of Scots, and for the sal-
' vation of my said umquhil husband's soul and
' mine: And also, for the salvation of the souls of
' those that shall put to their helping hand, or sall
' give any thing to this work: As also, for the
' patrons of the said chapel: And also, for the
' souls of all those of whom we have had any
' thing whilk we have not restored, and for the
' whilk we have not given satisfaction; to have
' given and granted, and by this my present char-
' ter in poor and perpetual alms, and to have con-
' firmed in mortification: As also, to give and
' grant, and by this present charter, gives in poor
' alms and mortification, to confirm to Almighty

'God, with the blessed Virgin Mary, the said
'chapell and chapell house, for the sustentation of
'ane secular chaplain, and seven poor men, and
'for the chaplain, and four poor brethren, to have
'their yearly food, and perpetual sustentation
'within the said hospital, and for buying of their
'habits every twa year once, I mortify these an-
'nualrents under-written; to wit, ane yearly an-
'nualrent of aughtscore and aught merks money
'of Scotland, out of that annualrent of threescore
'pounds yearly, to be uplifted and tane at twa
'terms yearly, Whitsunday and Martinmass in
'Winter, be equall portions, out of all and haill
'the barony of Carnwath miln, and pertinents
'thereof, and the other two merks of the said an-
'nualrent of threescore pound, to be applyed and
'used for my use, during my lifetime; and after
'my decease, to the poor brethren under-written:
'As also, for the dyet and sustentation of other
'three poor ones, and buying of their habites ilk
'twa year, after the decease of me the said Jonet,
'reserving to me my liferent, during my lifetime,
'viz The forsaid annualrent of twa merks of the
'threescore pounds yearly, to be uplifted out of the
'lands of Carnwath: as also, another yearly annu-
'alrent of twenty merks money of Scotland, yearly
'to be uplifted, as said is, out of all and haill the
'lands pertaining to Kathrine Gillespie and John
'Cockburn, her spouse, lyand in the burgh of Edin-

' burgh, upon the south-side of the high street
' thereof, betwixt the trans of the vennel called
' Hair's closs, and the trans of the vennel called
' Borthwick's closs: As also, ane other yearly an-
' nualrent of ten merks, out of the tenement of
' umquhile Andrew Harly, lying upon the north
' part of the King's high street: And also, ane
' other annualrent of twelve merks, out of the
' tenement of land pertaining to umquhile James
' Young: And also, another annualrent of thir-
' teen shillings and fourpence, out of the tene-
' ment of land pertaining to Edward Thomson,
' baxter, lying in the said burgh in Peebles-wynd.
' Whilk chaplain and his successors, shall have for
' their yearly sustentation twenty four merks
' money of Scotland, out of the foresaid yearly
' annualrent of aughtscore and aught merks, dure-
' ing Jonet Rynd's lifetime, and after her decease,
' out of all the foresaid yearly annualrents, to be
' taken up be himself at Whitsunday, and Martin-
' mass in Winter, every year in all time comeing,
' be equall portions. Whilk chaplain shall have
' the care, government and administration of the
' foresaid hospital, and of the foresaid poor bre-
' thren and all other poor brethren that shall, in
' any time thereafter, be put thereintill, and shall,
' three times in the year, provide to them the ec-
' clesiastical sacrament, providing they be found meet
' and apt for receaveing thereof; to wit, the feast

' of Pasch, Pentecost, and Nativity of our Lord Je-
' sus Christ. Whilk chaplane alse shall see, that in
' the foresaids feasts, and other convenient times,
' chiefly when they shall be sick of any heavie infir-
' mity, how the foresaid poor shall be worthyly dis-
' posed for receaveing of the sacrament; and for
' that effect, he shall exhort them, and shall chari-
' tably move them, and shall hear their confessions.
' And the said chaplain shall be obliged every fe-
' riat time of the week, if it be not ane feast day,
' to make ane mess of rest. with ane psalm direct
' to the LORD, for the foresaid souls. Neither
' shall it be leisome to the said chaplain to have
' any substitute under him, to serve in the said
' hospital for him, except in the time of infirmity
' and weakness allenerly; to the whilk mess the
' foresaid seven poor, and any others to be found
' thereintil to be present, and to interceed at GOD
' for the foresaid souls, and he sall have ane care,
' that the foresaid poor shall dilligently observe the
' whole foundation and articles as is herein sett
' down   And farder, We will and ordain, That
' the said chaplane and his successors for the time,
' at the first term of their entry and admission in
' the said hospitall, shall find sufficient caution to
' the patrons of the said hospital, for the well pre-
' servation of all the jewells, ornaments, and o-
' thers whatsomever, whilk fall belong to the said
' hospital, to be delivered be them to the patrons

' under an inventar; and that he shall not sell,
' nor put away any of the said ornaments, neither
' shall it be leisume to the said chaplane to embrace
' any other chaplanrie or ecclesiastick office; whilk
' if he doe, his chaplanrie shall vaik without any
' declarator of any judge, and it shall be leisume
' to the patrons to confer the samen upon ane o-
' ther. And if he be found incontinent of his bo-
' dy, either be lunary, adultery, incest, drunken-
' ness, dissentions, or of any other nottor or mani-
' fest crimes, and found culpable by the patrones,
' or most pairt of them, before ane nottor and
' faithful witnesses, shall be three times admonisht
' to desist frae them, and after ane full year out-
' run, he be found incorrigible, it shall be con-
' frrred be the patrons upon ane able chaplane.
' And farder, the said chaplane, every year, once
' in the year, for the said Michael and Jonet, sall
' make suffrages, which is, I am pleased, and di-
' rect me, O LORD, with ane mess of rest, be-
' ing naked, he cloathed me; with two wax can-
' dles burning on the altar. To the whilk suffra-
' ges and mess, he shall cause ring the chapel bell
' the space of ane quarter of an hour, and that all
' the foresaid poor, and others that shall be there-
' intill, shall be present at the foresaid mess with
  their habites, requesting all these that shall come
' in to hear the said mess to pray for the said souls.

E

' And farder, every day of the blessed Mary Mag-
' dallen, patron of the foresaid hospital, and the day
' of the indulgence of the said hospital, and every
' other day of the year, the said chaplaine shall
' offer up all the oblations, and for every oblation
' shall have twa wax candleds upon the altar, and
' twa at the foot of the image of the patron in
' twa brazen candlesticks, and twa wax torches
' on the feast of the nativity of our Saviour, Pasch,
' and Whitsunday, of the days of Mary Magdal-
' len, and of the days of the indulgences granted
' to the said hospital, and doubleing at other graet
' feasts, with twa wax candles alenerly. And
' likeways, he sall preserve the altar in the orna-
' ments thereof, and he sall preserve the jewells
' and ornaments of the said altar clean and tight,
' and he sall be obliged and restricted to furnish
' bread, wine and wax to the said hospital, for the
' haill year. As also, the said chaplain shall be
' obliged, at his entry, before he be admitted to
' the said hospital, to give his great oath, by touch-
' ing the sacred Evangile, that he shall neither
' directly nor indirectly, by whatsomever pretence
' or colier, seek the derogation of this foundation,
' in haill or in part, neither be himself nor be
' any other party; neither shall he have any dis-
' pensation or derogation from ony other the time
' of his admission; neither shall he be put into
' the said chaplanry be any other, but shall only

' have his admission from the saids patrons to
' the effect, that if he derogate any thing from
' the said hospital, and fall not fulfil the haill ar-
' ticles and clauses thereof, he sall be the same pa-
' trons be removed, and another able chaplain put
' in his place. And also, We will and declare,
' that the foresaid seven poor men, and likewise
' any other of that kind that shall be found it or
' put thereintil be any others, that they shall give
' obedience to the said chaplain, in all honest and
' leisome things, as their undoubted and lawful
' master of the said hospital; and that none be
' admitted amongst the said poor brethren of the
' said hospital, but such as are not married, and
' not stained with an concubine, or with any other
' notorious crime, and that none be admit-
' ted except he be past, before his admission, three-
' score years, except they be impotent and mi-
' serable persons, who otherways are not able to
' get their daily bread. And that no woman,
' howsoever miserable or impotent, be any ways re-
' ceived or admitted in the said hospital; and that
' no woman shall frequent this house of hospital
' at any time, and chiefly in the night time; and
' that one of the seven poor men, weekly, in his own
' turn, shall be janitor, who shall open and steik
' the gates thereof, and shall make clean the said
' chapel and common house thereof every day,

'and keep it honest from all filth. And if it
'chance that the said janitor be sick for the time,
'that he cannot do it, then ane other of the said
'poor brethren, in his turn most able and meet,
'by the discretion of the said chaplain, shall be
'appointed. And the said janitor, every day
'from Pasch to the feast of St. Jude, from half
'six in the morning, he shall open the gates, and
'close them again at aught hours at night; and
'the rest of the year he shall open at seven hours
'in the morning, and close them again at seven
'at night, and shall ring the bell of the said cha-
'pel for the space of a quarter of an hour, im-
'mediately after the opening, and a little before
'the closing: And that the seven poor, and every
'one of them, shall immediately after ringing of
'the bell, repeat the Lord's Prayer five times
'and the Angelical Salutation fifty times, and
'the Belief of the apostles once in the day; and
'they shall repeat the twa psalms that are
'called the *blessed Virgin's*, before compleating of
'their dinner, and refection at twelve hours.
'And the dinner being done, the foresaid haill
'poor, within the said hospital for the time, shall
'conveen before the great altar, and there, with
'their bowed knees, give five *Pater Nosters*, fifty
'*Ave Maria's*, and ane *Creed*, &c.'

The hospital was founded by Michel M'Quhan, Anno 1503; but the charter by the relict Anno 1545.

This chapel is adorned with the arms of the good town of Edinburgh, being argent, a castle triple towered sable, marshalled of the 1st, surmounted with thanes gules, supported on the dexter by a virgin lady, on the sinister with a deer, and accolee: Behind the shield the sword of honour, and mace ensigned with an Imperial Crown; below in a compartment, *Nisi Dominus Frustra.* Round this atchievement are the armorial ensigns of the following incorporations, according to their precedency.

In the first O·al.

I. CHIRURGEONS.

Az. on a fess. ar. a naked man fessways proper, betwixt a dexter hand palmed, and in its palm an eye proper, issuing from the chief. In the dexter canton a saltire ar under an Imperial Crown or, or proper, surmounted of a thistle proper or vert. and in base a castle ar. masoned sab. all within a border or, charged with the several instruments suitable to the society.

II. Goldsmiths.

Quarterly gu. and az. on the 1. a leopard's head or, 2d, a covered cup, and in chief 2 annulets or, 3 as 2, and 4 as 1.

III. Skinners.

Ermine on a chief gu. 3 Imperial Crowns or.

IV. Furriers.

Parted per fefs, gu. and ar. a pale countercharged of the fame on the 1ft 3 goats of the 2d.

V. Hammermen.

Az. a hammer proper, enfigned with an Imperial Crown.

VI. Wrights.

Az. a fquare and compafs or.

VII. Masons.

Ar. on a cheveron betwixt 3 towers embattelled fab. a compafs or.

VIII. Taylors.

Az. Sciffars expanded or.

IX. Baxters.

Az. 3 Garbs or, from the chief waved, a hand iffuing, holding a pair of ballances extending to the bafe.

X. Fleshers.

Ar. 2 flaughter axes proper faltire-ways, accompanied with 3 Cows heads couped fab. 2 in flank and 1 in bafe, and on a chief az. a boar's head couped betwixt 2 garbs or.

XI. Cordiners.

Az. their cutting knife in pale, and in chief, a ducal crown or.

XII. Websters.

Ar. on a chev. az. betwixt 3 leopards heads of the fame, holding in their mouths a fpool or fhuttle of yarn or, as many rofes gu.

XIII. Hatters and Waulkers.

Parted per pale gu. and ar. on the 1ft a chev. of the laft, betwixt two hatftring bands in chief, and in bafe a thiftle or, on the fecond, a finifter hand palmed proper, erected in pale betwixt 2 hatftrings fab. and in chief a hat of the laft.

XIV. Bonnetmakers and Litsters.

Ar. a fess betwixt 2 bonnets az. or proper, tufted gu. impaled with or, a chev. gu. betwixt 3 cushions az.

And round the hammermens arms, in a second oval, the ensigns of the following art:

XV. Blacksmiths.

Az. a chev. betwixt 3 hammers, each ensigned with ducal crowns or.

XVI. Cutlers.

Gu. 6 daggers placed saltire ways, 2 and 2, proper, handled or.

XVII. Saddlers.

Az. a chev. betwixt 3 saddles or.

XVIII. Locksmiths.

Az. a key impaled or.

XIX. Lorimers.

Az. a cheveron betwixt 3 horse-bridle bits ar.

XX. Armorers.

Arg. on a chev. gu. 4 swords saltire-ways, proper, handled or, and on a chief of the second, 2 helmets of the same.

XXI. Peutherers.

Az. on a chev. ar. betwixt 3 portculices or, as many thistles vert. and flowered gules.

XXII. Shearsmiths.

Gu. woolshears impaled az.

Placed above these arms are the imperial arms of Scotland, *thus blazoned,* viz.

Or, a lion ramp. gu. armed and languid az. within a double tressure, flowered and counter-flowered, with Flower de Lisses of the 2d, encircled with the order of Scotland, the same being composed of rue and thistles, having the image of St Andrew, with his cross on his breast, above the shield a helmet, answerable to his Majesty's high quality and jurisdiction, with a mantle or, doubled ermine, adorned with an imperial crown, beautified with crosses pattee, and Flower de Lisses, surmounted on the top, for his Majesty's crest, with a lion sejeant, full faced, gu. crowned or, holding in his dexter paw a naked sword proper, and in the sinister, a scepter, both erected pale ways, supported by two unicorns argent, crowned with imperial, and gorged with open crowns, to the laſt chains affixed, paſſing betwixt their fore legs, and reflexed over their backs or, he on the dexter imbracing and bearing up a banner of cloth of gold, charged with the royal arms of Scotland; on the ſiniſter, another banner azure, charged with the St. Andrew's croſs argent, both ſtanding on a compartment placed underneath, from which iſſues two thiſtles, one towards each ſide of the eſcutcheon and for motto in an eſcrol above all, in defence; under the table of the copartment, *Nemo me impune laceſſet.*

The hammermen's ſeal, is the effigies of St. Eloi in his apoſtolical veſtments proper, ſtanding in a church porch, a porch adorned with five pyramid ſteeples engraven, each ſurmounted with a plain croſs, holding in his dexter a hammer barways, and in the ſiniſter a key bend-ways. Round the effigies, are theſe words, *Sigillum commune Artis Tudiatorum.*

The above fundamental charter, in favours of the Magdalen hoſpital, is ſwelled with the popiſh doctrine of merit, and gives us a true repreſentation of the chicanery of Romiſh prieſts, who, to fill their coffers, and make their kitchen ſmoak, ſet heaven itſelf to ſale. The avarice of churchmen, in theſe dark times, as the learned ſir George

M'Kenzie in his printed pleadings obferves, was fo extravagant, that the legiflature in Germany, Denmark, and other countries, taxed the Quotas of pious donations, left the people, decoyed by their priefts to purchafe heaven, fhould have ftarved themfelves upon earth.

As the hammermen have St. Eloi and St. Mary Magdalen for their guardians; fo the Chirurgeons have St. Mungo, which appears by their feal of caufe, a copy of which follows:

'TILL all and fundry whas knawledge thir
' prefent letters fhall com, the provoft, bailies,
' and council of the burgh of Edinburgh, greeting
' in God everlafting, wit your univerfitys that
' the day of the date of thefe prefents, compeired
' before Us fittaind in judgement in the Tolbuith
' of the faid burgh, the kirk mafter *, and brether
' of the furgeons and barbaris within the fame,
' and prefented to us their bill and fupplication,
' defiring us, for the loving of God, honor of our
' foveraign lord, and all his leidges, and for wor-
' fhipe and policy of this burgh, all for the guid
' rule and order to be had and made amongft the
' faids crafts in tyme to come, that we wauld grant,
' and confent to them the priviledges, ruls and

---

* Deacon, or chief mafter of the incorporation.

' ſtatuts contained in the ſaid bill and ſupplication,
' qlk after follows:

‘ TO you my lord provoſt, baillies, and worthy
‘ council of this guid toune, right humblie means
‘ and ſhaws, your dayly ſervitors the kirk maſter
‘ and brether of the ſurgeons and barbars within
‘ this brughe, that where we believe it is weall
‘ knawne till all yor wiſdoms, how that we uphald
‘ an altar ſituate within the colledge kirk of St.
‘ Giles, in the honour of God and St. Mungo our
‘ patrone, and has nae importance to uphauld the
' ſame, but our ſober oukleye penny and upſets,
‘ qulks are ſmall in effect till ſuſtance and uphald
‘ our ſaid altar in all neceſſary things convenient
‘ thereto. And becauſe we ar, and ever wes of
‘ guid mynd to do this guid toune all the ſtede
‘ pleaſure and ſervice that we cane or may, baith
' in walking, warding, ſtenting, and bearing of
‘ all portable charges within this brugh at all tyms,
‘ as other nightbours and crafts does within the
‘ ſame. We deſire at your lordſhips and wiſdoms,
‘ till give and grant till us, and our ſucceſſors, the
‘ rules, ſtatuts and priviledges underwritten, qhilk
‘ ar conſonant to reaſon, honor to our ſoveraign
‘ lord, and all his leidges profit, and love to this
' guid town.

‘ IN the firſt, That we might haue yearly choſne

of the BLUE BLANKET. 63

‘ amongſt us, our kirk maſter and over man, to
‘ whom the haill brethren of the crafts foreſaids
‘ ſhall obey for that year.

‘ 2do. *Item*, That nae maner of perſon occupy
‘ nor uſe any poynts of our ſaid crafts of ſurgery,
‘ or barber craft, within this brugh, but gif he
‘ be firſt frie man and burges of the ſamen, and
‘ that he be worthy and expert in all the poynts
‘ belongand to the ſaids crafts, diligently and a-
‘ viſedly examined, and admitted by the maſters
‘ of the ſaid crafte, for the honorable ſerving of
‘ our ſaid ſovereign lord, his lieges, and night-
‘ bours of this brugh : And alſe, that every man
‘ that is to be made frie man among us, be exa-
‘ mined and provit in thir points following ; that
‘ is to ſay, that

‘ He knaw anatomia, natur and complexion of
‘ every member of humans body ; and lykwiſe
‘ that he knaw all the veins of the ſamen, that he
‘ may maik phlebothomia in due tyme, and alſe
‘ that. And alſe, That he knaw in quhilk mem-
‘ ber the ſign hes domination for the tyme ; for e-
‘ ver ilk man aught to knaw the natur and ſub-
‘ ſtance of every thing he wirks, or elſe he's ne-
‘ gligent ; and that we may haue anes in the year
‘ ane condempait man after he be dead, to maik

F

' anatamia of wherthrow we may haue experience
' ilk ane to inſtruct others, and we ſhall do ſuffer-
' age for the ſaul.

' 3to, And that nae barbar maſter nor ſervant
' within this burgh, hant, uſe nor exerce the craft
' of ſurgery, without he be expert, and knaw per-
' fectly the things aboue written; and quhat per-
' ſons that ſhall happen to be admitted frie men or
' maſters to the ſaids crafts, or occupys any part of
' the ſame ſhall pay at his entrie for his upſet, five
' pounds uſual money of Scotland, to the repara-
' tion and uphalding of our ſaid altar of St.
' Mungo, for divyne ſervice to be done thereat,
' with a dinner to the maſters of the ſaids crafts
' at his admiſſion and entreſs amangſt us; except
' and that every frie man maſter of the ſaid crafts,
' one of his lawful gottne ſons to be frie of any
' money peying, except the dinner to be made to
' the maſters, after he be examined and admitted
' by them, as ſaid is.

' 4to, *Item* That nae maſter of the ſaids crafts
' ſhall taik any apprentice or ſied man in tyme
' coming, till uſe the ſurgeon craft, without he
' can baith writt and reade.

' And the ſaid maſter of any of the ſaids crafts
' that taiks any printice ſhall pay at his entrie to

'the reparation of the said altar, twenty shillings,
'and that nae master of the saids crafts, recept or
'receive any other masters prentice, or servant,
'quhillt the issue of his tearms be runne, and
'wha that does in the contrair thereof, as aftan as
'he faills, shall pay twenty shillings to the repa-
'ration of the said altar, but favours.

'5*to*, *Item*, Every master that is received frie
'man to the saids crafts, shall pay his oukly pen-
'ny with the priests myte, as he shall happen to
'come about, and every servand that is a fied man,
'to the masters of the saids crafts, shall pay ilk
'ouk ane half penny to the said altar, and repara-
'tions thereof; and that we haue power till choyse
'a chaplaine till do divyn service dayly at aur said
'altar at all tymes, when the same should wawyik
'[*be vacant*], and till choyce an officer till pafs
'with us for the engathering of our quarter pay-
'ments, and oukly pennys, and to pafs before us
'on *corpus* [*Christi*] XI day, and the otteus [*octa-
'ves*] thereof, and all other general proceffions
'and gatherings, siklyk, as other crafts hes with-
'in this brugh, and that ane of the masters of the
'foresaids crafts, with the chaplain and officer of
'the same, pafs at all tyms needful lift and raise
'the said quarter payments frae every person that
'awe the same; and gif any disobeys, that we

' may poynd and diftrenzie therefor all tyms,
' hauing an officer of the town with us.

' *6to, Item,* That nae perfon nor frie man of
' the faids crafts, purchace any lordfhips in con-
' trair the rules and ftatutes above-written, in
' hendring or fkaithing of the crafts forfaid, or
' common weall thereof, under the pain of tinfel
' [*lofing*] of their freedoms.

' *7mo, Item,* That all the mafters, frie men and
' brether of the faids crafts readily obey, and
' come to their kirk mafter, or deacon, at all tyms,
' quhen they fhall be required thereto by the faid
' officer, for till hear quarter compts, or till avife
' for any thing concerning the common weall of
' the faids crafts ; and wha that difobeys, fhall pay
' 20 s. to the reparation of the faid altar; and that
' nae perfons, man nor woman within this brugh,
' maik nor fell any aquavitæ within the famen, ex-
' cept the faid maifters, brether, and frie men
' of the faid crafts, under the pain of efcheat of
' the famen, but favours. Befeeking

' Heirfor your lordfhips and wifdoms, at the
' reverence of God, that ye will avyze with thir
' our fimple defyrs, ruls, ftatuts and priviledges
' above-writtne, and grant us the fame ratifyd and
' approven by yow, under yor comon feall of caufe;

' and with the grace, we shall do sik service and
' pleasur to the king's grace, and the good, that
' ye shall be contentit thereof; and yor deliver-
' ance heiruntil humbly I beseek.

' THE quhilk bill of supplication, with the
' rul, statuts and priviledges contind therintill,
' beand read before us in judgment; and we
' therewith beand riplie and distinctly adysed,
' thinks the same consonant to reason, and nae
' hurt to our sovereign lord's hynes, us, nor nan
' other of his leidges, therintill: And therefor
' we consent and grant the samen to the forsaids
' crafts of surgenary and barbars, and to their suc-
' cessors. And in suae far as we may, and hes
' pouer, confirms, ratifys and approves the saids
' statuts, ruls, and priviledges in all poynts and
' artikls contind in the said supplication above-
' writtne. And this to all and sundry quhom it
' effeirs, or may effeir, we maik knawne by thir
' our letters; and for the mair verification and
' streanth of the samen, we haw too hungen our
' comon seall of cause.' At Edinburght 1st July,
the zear of God, 1505.

The seal of the good town is appended with
this inscription round it.

Sigilum burgi de Edr. ad causus.

THE crafts, who behaved so loyally before they were incorporate, and formed into societies, continued to flourish in their sovereign's favours, and were warmed with beams from the throne; a signal instance of their fidelity to King James V. I cannot miss to relate. The crown being debitor to the town of Edinburgh in vast sums, for which she had not only the security of the government, but the personal obligations of the monarch; wearied with disappointments, and the merchants murmuring for want of payment from the town, to whom they had given considerable loans, for the behoof of the publick; the magistrates, and merchants in concert, raised a mob, and gave directions to the ring-leaders, what, and how far to act, to insult the King as he was passing the streets to the parliament house; who, after a scuffle with his guards, violently seized upon his sacred Majesty, and thrust him within the walls of their common gaol: Some of his Majesty's retinue having alarmed the deacons of crafts with what had happened, the trades instantly conveened, and unanimously agreed, that their ensign should be displayed, for convocating the lieges, to rescue their captive monarch; which was accordingly done, and soon procured him to be liberate, and safely conveyed to his royal palace of Holyrood-house. The magistrates, who had hounded out the mob, dreading the consequence of their traiterous actings, and knowing the weak side of Cuthbert the deacon conveener, who headed the trades, bribed him by a lusty purse of Gold, to betray his trust.

The King next morning sent for Cuthbert, (whom he called his faithful general) and told him, he had a grateful remembrance of the loyalty and valour of his faithful subjects the trades of Edinburgh, and was resolved to confer some remarkable token of favour upon them.

Cuthbert, well instructed by the magistracy and merchant council how to behave, answered,

MAY it please your excellent majesty, *we your obliged and devoted servants the* trades *of* Edinburgh, *did nothing but what was our bounden duty: But since your Majesty is graciously pleased not only to remember, but reward our dutiful behaviour, I presume, in name of my brethren, to beseech your* sacred majesty, *to make your most faithful and loyal servants the* trades *of* Edinburgh, *in all time coming, free of that toilsome affair of being magistrates of the burgh, and let the disloyal merchants be henceforth loaded with the office.*

The King surprized with the supplication, gave a smile, and said, Cuthbert, It shall be done.

The man's treachery was soon blown about, to the amazement of the incorporations, who found, that their loyaly, which they justly expected would have advanced their interest, as it did their honour, had turned to their real detriment: And therefore they applied to the courtiers, to represent to his majesty, how villaniously they had had been betrayed. As soon as the King was informed, he commanded the crafts to lay their demands before him, which they accordingly did in a short memorial, craving his majesty would be pleased to confirm all their ancient privileges of the *Blue Blanket*. His Majesty graciously received their petition; and not only granted their request, corroborating all former grants, and privileges by immemorial possession; but considerably enlarged its authority, declaring, that whenever they displayed their ensign of the *Blue Blanket*, either in defence of the crown, or crafts, all craftsmen in Scotland, and soldiers in the King's pay, who had been educate in a trade, should repair to that standard, and fight under the command of their general. Thus did that excellent monarch reward loyalty, and the treacherous conveener was murdered at the North Loch, near a well, yet known by the name of Cuthbert's well.

This was certainly the highest honour the King could put upon the crafts: for a standard hath been esteemed so in all ages. Hence the scripture expresses the strength and power of the Church by a standard, *Cant.* vi. 4. *Thou art beautiful, O my love, as Tirzah, comely as Jerusalem, terrible as an army with banners,* and the love and favour of God. Cant ii. 4. *He brought me into the banqueting house, and his banner over me was love.* Cant. v. 10. According to the Hebrew text, *My beloved is the standard-bearer among ten thousand;* which our translators very defectively render, *The chief among't ten thousand.* And the antiquity and honour of the standard is more plainly expressed in the book of numbers, ii. 2, &c. *Every man of the tribe of Israel shall pitch by his own standard, with the ensign of their father's house, far off, about the tabernacle of the congregation shall they pitch, and on the east side, toward the rising of the sun shall they of the standard of the camp of Judah pitch throughout their armies, and Naashon, the son of Amminadab, shall be captain of the children of Judah. On the west side shall be the standard of the camp of Ephraim, according to their armies, and the captain of the sons of Ephraim shall be Elishama, the son of Ammihud. The standard of the camp of Dan shall be on the north side, by their armies,* &c.

As the Almighty has compared the power of his Church to, and honoured his saints with, a standard; so hath it been the custom in all ages of the world, for generous princes, in rewarding valour and noble atchievements, to confer a ftandard, as Guillim in his difplay of heraldry obferves, Hungus, King of Picts, gave to his wariors an enfign, bearing the figure of a crofs, in the fafhion of a faltire. Philip King of France (or as Favin would have it) Baldwin the firft, King of Jerufalem, gave to his followers an enfign, with two red croffes united unto one; and to the Chriftian merchants of Naples, who fought againft the Saracens for the Chriftian religion, whom he made knights of Rhodes, now of Malta, a white crofs, to be worn on their left fhoulder. Reme duke of Anjou, King of Jerufalem and Sicily, gave to his warriors an enfign of crimfon velvet, with a golden crefcent, and enamelled red, becaufe they had been long dyed in blood. Arthur King of the Britains (as Seger remarks) founder of the order of the round table, inftitute the fraternity of the knights of the table, in token of brotherly love, gave them a round table, which yet hangs in their caftle: And to give no more inftances, Sir John Smith got from King Charles I. the royal ftandard which he carried off at the battle of Edgehill, and was knighted under it.

Since Kings in all ages have beftowed the enfign upon well-deferving perfons, we need not wonder that the Kings of Scotland, to whofe blood generosity is congenial, bestowed this standard of the *Blue Blanket* upon tradesmen, who rendered themselves noble by their actions, As Diogenes says, ' Nobleness of blood is a cloak of sloth, and ' a vizard of cowardice; but immortal is their ' fame upon whom princes confer honours, accord- ' ing to their deserts, for defending the holy ' Church, King or country.' And what reason can be assigned why tradesmen should not be advanced as well as others, since the greatest princes on earth have been artists. Henry Peocham tells, that Solyman the Magnificent, his trade was making of arrows. In Venice every artificer is a magnifico. In the low countries, mechanicks are declared gentlemen, by a grant from King Charles V. in consideration of their services, during his wars. And to all those who contemn mechanicks, who raise themselves by their valour, I must give the memorable answer of Verduge a Spaniard, and a general in Friezland, to some persons of quality, who resented his taking the head of the table at a publick entertainment. ' Gentlemen, ' question not my birth, (though I be the son of a ' hangman) for I am the son of my own desert and ' fortune. If any man do as much as I have done, ' let him take the table head with all my heart.'

Thus far have I traced the loyalty of the crafts of Edinburgh, and shall now proceed to the reign of

Mary Queen of Scots,

during whose minority, a controversy being betwixt the magistrates of Edinburgh and the deacons of crafts, for breaking in upon the legal privileges of the incorporations; which so inflamed the deacons of the trades with a keen resentment, that in the tolbooth of Edinburgh, where the courts of justice then sat, they drew their swords, demanding justice; and if they had not been restrained by the King's forces then in the city, whom the magistrates called to their assistance, they had been killed on the bench.

Being thus relieved, they committed the assassins, as they termed them, prisoners to the castle of Edinburgh, where they remained in close confinement, till the several incorporations having met in the absence of their deacons, and concluded to relieve them, after the never-failing method of displaying the *Blue Blanket*, which they did, and thereby convocated thousands of the King's lieges in a very few hours.

The extraordinary concourse of people alarmed the government so, that the King's privy council met upon the extraordinary emergent, and resolved, that the earl of Arran should interpose his royal authority, and ſtop procedure of the lords of juſticiary, before whom was a criminal proceſs intented at the inſtance of the ſaids magiſtrates of Edinburgh, againſt the deacons of crafts, and to importune the differences betwixt them to be ſubmitted to him. The wiſe regent complied with the advice, and publiſhed the following edict.

Gubernator,

'JUSTICE and juſtice clerk, and zour de-
' putis, We greit zow weille, FORSAEMEIKLE-
' AS, William Smeberd, Robert Hutchieſoune,
' James Forret, Thomas Schort, Archbald Dew-
' ar, Andro Edgar, George Ritchardſone, Thom-
' as Ramſay, James Downwieke, William Purdie,
' William Quhite, being in warde, within the
' caſtle of Edinburgh, for alleaged drawing of
' quhinzearis in the tolbuith of Edinburgh, in
' preſence of the provoſt and baillies thairof, the
' xi day of Auguſt inſtant, and furth-bringing
' of the *Blew Banner* of the *Blew Blankett* in our
' preſence, callit, The *Hally Guiſt*, has foundin
' ſuretie to underlye the law for the ſamyne, and
' for all otheris crymes that can be impute to them
' the x. day of October nixt to cum, as the act of
' adjournal maid thairupon beirs: Howbeit, as
' we are informit, the ſaidis perſonis are innocent
' of the ſaids alleagit crimis. OUR WILL IS

'HEIRFORE, and for certain uthiris reasonable causes and considerationis moveing us, we charge zow strictly and commandis, that incontinent, efter the sicht hereof, ze desist and seiss frae all preceeding agains the saids persons, or ony o- thiris craftismen of the saids burgh, for the saidis allegett crymes, till the day above written; or for ony otheris crimes, actionis, transgressio- ouis, crymis, or offencess quhatsomever, comit- it or done be thame, or ony of thame in ony time bygane unto the day of the date hereof; but continowe the samyn to the third day of the air.' Discharging zow othirwayes theirof, and of zour offices in that parte in the mene tyme be thir presentis, notwithstanding ony writtingis gevin, or to be givene in the contraire, or ony pains contenit therein, as ze will answer to us theirupon. Subscrivit with our hand, and ge- vine under our signet at Haly-rude house, the first day of September, the zeir of God one thousand five hundred and forty three zeirs.

JAMIS G.

Thus, the crafts defended the rights and liber- ties of the *Blanket* to the exposing of their lives; for they could not bruik the unjust proceedings of the magistrates, and therefore determined to keep them intire, which they had obtained by an infi- nite multitude of great actions.

I must here take occasion to remove a common objection against the authority of the *Blue Blanket*, that it never had any legal privileges: For, had not the regent known, that the crafts were warranted to display their colours when the privileges of their incorporations were violate, he would surely have done justice to the magistrates, in punishing these crafts as a seditious rabble, and with the power of the Queen's forces, reduced them to obedience, especially the deacons, by whose authority the lieges were convocate, who were prisoners within the King's garrison: But it is remarkable, though the banner was displayed in his own presence, as his edict relates, he did not punish them for a trespass against law, but was forced to have a recourse to policy, to stop the effusion of Christian blood, by interpelling the judges of justiciary from proceeding against them for their riot, in assaulting the magistracy in their court of justice with weapons; for doing of which they were certainly culpable, and therefore he obliged them to find bail as to that. We must undoubtedly conclude, they justified their actings in displaying the *Blanket*, otherwise there had certainly been a law enacted, prohibiting them from that practice, for the future, under the pain of high treason.

Though the crafts and other citizens of Edin-

burgh made a bold ſtand for the glorious reformation, (which was carried on in the reign of this beautiful, learned, but unfortunate lady, Queen Mary, who tenaciouſly adhered to the intereſt of the Romiſh church) in a more tumultuary way than in England, and other reformed countries: Yet had they a juſt ſenſe of their obedience to Cæſar, and acted under the influence of that Chriſtian maxim *, 'That it is the duty of the people to pray for magi‐
' ſtrates, to honour their perſons, pay them tribute,
' obey their lawful commands, to be ſubject to their
' authority for conſcience ſake; and that infidelity
' and difference in religion doth not make void the
' magiſtrates juſt and legal right, nor free the people
' from due obedience to them.' So that their actions, during this reign, when turbulent factions were bandying one another, ſhowed a venerable *decorum*. And the Queen was ſenſible of their loyalty, as is evident from the preamble of a charter granted by her, and Henry her huſband, under her great ſeal, to the provoſt, council, and communities of the ſaid burgh, and their ſucceſ‐ſors, ' Of all and haill the ſuperiority of the vil‐
' lage of Leith, with the pertinents and ſuperiori‐
' ty of the inhabitants and indwellers of the ſamen,
' as of the houſes, tenements, annualrents, links,
' orchards, profits, duties, ſervices, tenants, ten‐

---

* Weſtminſter Confeſſion of Faith, chap. 23. ſect. 4.

' andries, services of free tenants, &c.' As is at more length exprest in the said infeoffment, dated the 4th day of October 1565, and the 1st and 23d years of their reign. Which superiority of Leith, the magistrates of Edinburgh, by a letter of reversion, disponed back to the said Queen Mary, under reversion of ten thousand merks usual money of Scotland. This superiority of Leith was thereafter, by her son and successor King James VI. assigned to his beloved counseller Sir John Maitland of Thirleston his chancellor and secretary, his heirs and assignies, dated the 7th of July 1587, ratified and approven by the states of parliament the 29th day of the month and year foresaid; which reversion, is renounced by John Lord Thirleston, son and heir to the said Sir John Maitland, with advice and consent of Sir John Cockburn of Clarkingtoun his tutor testamentor, in favours of the provost, bailies, council, deacons of crafts, and community of the said burgh of Edinburgh, as is at length contained in the saids letters of renunciation, of the date the 28th of December 1607, and ratified by the said John Lord Thirlestoun, to the saids provost, bailies, council, deacons of crafts, and community of the said burgh, the 24th of November 1614.

The loyal crafts of Edinburgh gave surprising evidences of their loyalty to their King, and gratitude for the privileges of the *Blue Blanket*, during the long and peaceful reign of the first proteſtant King of Scotland, (who with learning and eloquence defended the reformation againſt cardinal Robert Bellarmine, one of the ſtouteſt pillars of the Romiſh hierarchy, and ſhowed how well he merited the royal title, defender of the faith.)

But before I proceed to this reign, I muſt relate two remarkable paſſages relating to the crafts, which I had almoſt omitted.

When faction and tumult poſſeſſed an abſolute and unlimited ſway, during this Queen's reign, the loyalty of the crafts was not at all diminiſhed: for when the Queen had recourſe to arms, to oppoſe the Earl of Murray and his aſſociates, who, under pretence of bringing the Earl of Bothwel, her huſband, to a fair trial, as acceſſary to the late King Henry's murder, had, Anno 1567, raiſed an army againſt her, and made her priſoner at Carberry-hill; ſhe was brought to Edinburgh; where, in ſtead of allowing her the uſe of her palace, ſhe was ſhut up in the provoſt's houſe. As ſhe entered the city, covered with tears and duſt, and in a garb far below her birth and merit, and inſulted by the mob, who cried, *Burn the whore:* * *burn the parricide.* This ſhe bore with

---

* Crawford's Memoirs, p. 38. and Melvill's Memoirs, p. 84.

fortitude of mind becoming a Chriſtian, and a Queen; but next morning, when ſhe opened the windows, and beheld not only ſtrong guards placed before the entry to the houſe, but a banner diſplayed on the ſtreet, on which was painted her dead huſband, King Henry, beneath the ſhade of a tree, with the young prince by his ſide, and the motto, *Judge and revenge my cauſe, O LORD*, ſhe burſt into tears, and complained againſt the affronts ſhe received, begging the people to compaſſionate her, now become a captive. The honeſt crafts, joined with other loyal citizens, pierced with pity to ſee their ſovereign thus uſed, and their enſign diſplayed, where the enſign of the *Blue Blanket* uſed to be erected in the cauſe of loyalty, crowded to the place, and compelled the conſpirators to reſtore her to the palace of Holy-roodhouſe.

I MUST indeed, as a faithful hiſtoriographer, relate that, Anno 1571, when the aſſociators againſt the Queen held a parliament in the Canongate, the city of Edinburgh being poſſeſſed by the loyaliſt troops, the crafts, who believed their religion to be in eminent danger, diſplayed the *Blue Blanket* (which, in ancient times, they were in uſe to do for the defence of religion) at the town of Leith, as Mr Crawford, Hiſtoriographer to Queen Anne, relates it, in his memoirs of the affairs of

Scotland, during the reign of Queen Mary, p. 210. 'The citizens, who either liked not the 'Queen, or the new magistrates, went off in an 'intire body to Leith, and set up their own stan- 'dard; upon which was written, in golden let- 'ters, *For God and the King;* and vanquished the 'loyalists.'

I now proceed to the reign of King JAMES VI. of Scotland, and I. of England.

The city of Edinburgh gave the highest testimonies of their love and loyalty to their infant sovereign that they were capable of, and opposed the earl of Morton regent, who ruled the roast, and over awed the young King's inclinations to mercy. Morton, to gain the affections of the citizens of Edinburgh, Anno 1579, caused summon a parliament to meet at Edinburgh, and the King to leave Stirling, where formerly parliaments were held When his Majesty, upon his journey to the capital city, came near the West port, he alighted from his horse, and a stately canopy of purple coloured velvet being held over his head, he received the magistrates of the city, who came bare headed all the way without the gate; within the gate stood Solomon, with a numerous train in Jewish habits, with the two women contending for the child, as is recorded, 1 Kings iii.

of the BLUE BLANKET. 83

As his Majesty ascended the West-bow, there hung down from the arch of the old port a large globe of polished brass, out of which a little boy, cloathed like a Cupid, descended in a machine, and presented him with the keys of the city all made of massy silver, and very artificially wrought; an excellent concert of music all the while accompanying the action.

When he came down the high street as far as the tolbooth, Peace, Plenty, and Justice met him, and harangued him in Greek, Latin, and Scottish languages. Opposite to the great Church stood Religion, who addressed him in the Hebrew tongue: upon which he was pleased to enter the Church, where Mr. Lawson, a Presbyterian divine, made a learned discourse in behalf of these of the reformed religion.

When his Majesty came out, Bacchus sat mounted on a gilded hogshead at the market cross, distributing wine in large bumpers, the trumpets all the while sounding, and the people crying, *God save the King.* At the east gate was erected his Majesty's nativity, and above that, the genealogies of all the Scots Kings, from Fergus I. All the windows were hung with pictures and rich tapestry, the streets strowed with flowers, and the cannon firing from the caftle, till his Majefty reached his palace.

Notwithstanding all this pomp and ceremony, which expreffed the love and reverence both clergy and laity bore to his facred Majefty, there was a fudden change of affairs. For,

Presbyterian government was eftablifhed in the church of Scotland, Anno, 1592, † which, it is probable. the wife King would not have altered, had not the Englifh clergy influenced him to admit thoughts of reftoring Epifcopacy; which the Scots clergy perceiving, ftrove to oppofe his purpofe, and ftrengthen their own intreft. New debates arifing grew to that hight, that in the year 1596, fome noblemen, barons, and minifters being affembled at Edinburgh, and perceiving, that the procefs laid againft Mr. David Black, who was profecute before the privy council for feditious fermons, as then termed, and ftirring up the people againft their Sovereign, wronged the privileges of their ecclefiaftic difcipline; and withal, being difpleafed at the clemency fhown to the Popifh Lords, were filled with refentment.

The King having diffolved the commiffion of

---

† Bifhop Guthry's Memoirs.

the General Assembly by his royal proclamation *, declaring it an unlawful convocation. The commission resolved, 'That since they were conveened by CHRIST's warrant to see into the good of the church, *Et ne quid Ecclesia detrimenti caperet*, they should continue;' and sent some of their number to the Octavians, (that was the title commonly given to the eight counsellors that were trusted with the King's affairs) to advertise them of the church's troubles, proceeding from their counsels, and thereafter petitioned the King himself, which was rejected, and a protestation entered against the refusal; but some noblemen, with Mr. Robert Bruce, having procured access to his Majesty, Mr. Robert said, They were sent by the noblemen and barons to bemoan the dangers threatened to religion, by the King's dealings against the true professors. What dangers do you discover? said the King. Under communing, said the other, our best affected people. that tender religion, are discharged the town. The King asked, who they were that durst conveen against his proclamation? The Lord-Lindsay replied, they durst do more than so, and that they would not suffer religion to be overthrown. Numbers of people were, by this time, thronging unmannerly into the room; whereupon the King not making any answer, arose, and went where the judges sat com-

---

* Spotiswood's Church History.

manding the doors to be shut. They that were sent to the King returning to the church, told, that that they were not heard; and that therefore they were to think of some other course. No course, said the Lord Lindsay, but let us stay together who are here, to stand fast to one another, and advertise our friends and favourers of religion to come in to us: For it shall be either theirs or ours. In consequence of this concert, they pitched upon the Lord Claud Hamilton to be their head, and dispatched a letter to him signed by Mr. Robert Bruce, and Mr. Walter Balcanqual, to come with diligence and accept the charge: but the fury of the multitude who attended that meeting, heated by the Lord Lindsay's unhappy expression, did not suffer them to wait upon the General's coming, but presently leapt to arms. Some cried, *Bring out Haman;* others cried, *The sword of the Lord and of Gideon; the day shall be theirs or ours.* And so great was the zeal of the unwary populace, that taking their march, they went straight towards the tolbooth of Edinburgh, where the King and his council were then sitting, and would have forced open the doors, which, upon the noise of the tumult, were shut, had not his Majesty's standerd bearer, John Wat, deacon conveener of the trades, drawn up, his lads, the soldiers of the *Blue Blanket,* and kept the rabble back till their fever cooled, and the Earl of Mar, from the castle, sent a company of musqueteers to guard the King, which his lieutenant quickly brought down the Castle-bank to the Grass-market, and from thence marched to the foot of Forrester's-wynd, and entering by the back stairs, came, where the King was; then the King commanded to open the doors, and advanced to the street. Upon notice whereof, Sir Alexander Home of North-berwick, provost of Edinburgh, with the crafts, convoyed the King to his royal palace at Holy-rood-house; from whence, next morning, he went to Linlithgow, where he swore, ‘ Had it not been for the loyalty of the ‘ crafts, he would have burnt the town of Edin- ‘ burgh, and salted it with salt.

By the stedfast adherence of the crafts to their Sovereign, even when they did not approve of, but were sorry for his actings, our capital city was preserved from destruction, as by their behaviour afterwards, it flourished in his favours.

On the last of that month of December, the King came to Leith, and staid there all night, giving orders for his entry into the town of Edinburgh next morning, which he did, and called for the magistrates, to hear what they had to say for the late tumult; who, in obedience to his Majesty's commands, compeared before him and his courti-

H

ers, and cleared themselves to his Majesty's conviction. For Spotiswood tells us, That,

Sir Alexander Home, provost, Rodger M'Math, George Todrick, Patrick Cochran, and Alexander Hunter, bailies, with a number of the town-council, falling down on their knees before the King, presented the following offers

' That for pacifying his Majesty's wrath, and
' satisfying the Lords of council, they should, up-
' on their oath, purge themselves of all know-
' ledge, or partaking in the said tumult; and as
' they had already made a diligent search to find
' out the authors; so they should not cease, until
' they had brought the trial to the utmost point;
' or, if his Majesty and council should think fit to
' take the examination, they should willingly re-
' sign their places to such as his Highness would ap-
' point, and assist him according to their power:
' And, because his Majesty had taken that tumult
' to proceed from certain sermons preached by
' their ministers, they should be expelled the city,
' never to return, without his Majesty's warrant.'
Upon which, the King was reconciled to them.

Thus the crafts behaved as loyally at this juncture, as they did during the troubles occasioned by the Earl of Bothwel, when the King was assaulted in his palace of Holy-rood-houfe, which obliged him to cry aloud from the windows, Treafon, Treafon.

The report of the accident going to the city of Edinburgh, the citizens went to arms, and made towards the palace to give the King relief, who fhowed himeflf from a window to the people, gave them thanks for their readinefs, and defired them to return to their dwellings. As the citizens gave repeated inftances of their valour and loyalty to the King, while he refided amongft us, fo after his acceffion to the throne of England, and when he returned to his native country, Scotland, and made his entry into Edinburgh, 16 of May 1617, joy appeared in every one of their countenances; they were ready to cry out in the words of Ben Johnfton's magnetick lady.

Now let our longing eyes enjoy their feaft,
And fill of thee, our fair fhap'd God-like man.
Thou art a banquet unto all our fenfes;
Thy form doth feaft our eyes, thy voice our ears,
As if we felt it ductile thro' our blood.

This paffionate love is gracefully expreft by the famous poet and orator, William Drummond of

Hathornden, in his speech to the King, in name of the town of Edinburgh.

'SIR, If nature could suffer rocks to move
'and abandon their natural places, this town,
'founded on the strength of rocks, (now by the
'clearing rays of your Majesty's presence, taking
'not only motion but life) had, with her castle,
'temples, and houses, moved towards you, and
'beseeched you to have acknowledged her your's,
'and her indwellers your most humble and affec-
'tionate subjects; and to believe how many souls
'are within her circuits, so many lives are devoted
'to your sacred person and crown. And here,
'SIR, she offers, by me, to the altar of your glo-
'ry, whole hecatombs of most hearty desires,
'praying all things may prove prosperous to you,
'that every virtue and heroic grace which make
'a prince eminent, may, with a long and blessed
'government, attend you; your kingdoms flourish-
'ing abroad with bays, at home with olives.
'Presenting you, SIR, who art the strong key of
'this little world of Britain, with these keys,
'which cast up the gates of her affection, and de-
'sign you power to open all the springs of the
'hearts of those her most loyal citizens: Yet this
'almost were not necessary: For as the rose, at
'the fair approach of the morning sun, displays
'and spreads her purples; so, at the very noise o

' your happy return to this your native country,
' their hearts, if they could have shined through
' their breasts, were with joy and fair hopes,
' made spacious, nor did they ever, in all parts,
' feel a more comfortable heat, than the glory of
' your presence at this time darts upon them.

' THE old forget their age, and look fresh and
' young, at the appearance of so gracious a prince;
' the young bear a part in your welcome, desiring
' many years of life, that they may serve you long.
' All have more joys than tongues: For as the
' words of other nations go far beyond, and sur-
' pass the affections of their heart; so, in this na-
' tion, the affection of their hearts is far above all
' they can express by words. Deign then, SIR,
' from the highest of Majesty, to look down on
' their lowness, and embrace it, accept the hom-
' age of their humble minds, accept their great
' good will, which they have ever carried to the
' high deserts of your ancestors, and shall ever to
' your own, and your royal race whilst these
' rocks shall be overshadowed with buildings,
' buildings inhabited by men; and while men
' be indued either with counsel or courage, or en-
' joy any piece of reason, sense, or life.

THIS speech was followed by another, delivered at the West port of Edinburgh, when his Majesty entered, by Mr. John Hay, town-clerk depute.

'HOW joyful your Majesty's return (gracious
' and dread Sovereign) is to this your native town,
' from that kingdom, due to your sacred person,
' by royal descent, the countenances and eyes of
' your Majesty's loyal subjects speak for their
' hearts. This is that happy day of our new birth,
' ever to be retained in fresh memory, with con-
' sideration of the goodness of Almighty G O D
' considered, with the acknowledgment of the
' same, acknowledged with admiration, admired
' with love, and loved with joy; wherein our
' eyes behold the greatest humane felicity our
' hearts could wish, which is to feed upon the
' royal countenance of our true Phœnix, the
' bright star of our Northern firmament, the or-
' nament of our age, wherein we are refreshed
' and revived with the heat, and bright beams of
' our sun, (the powerful adamant of our wealth)
' by whose removing from our hemisphere, we
' were darkned, deep sorrow and fear possessing
' our hearts, (without envying of your Majesty's
' happiness and felicity) our places of solace ever
' giving a new heat to the fever of the languish-
' ing remembrance of our happiness; the very
' hills and groves, accustomed of before to be re-

'freshed with the dew of your Majesty's presence,
'not putting on their wonted apparel, but with
'pale looks representing their misery for the de-
'parture of their royal King.

'I MOST humbly beg pardon of your most sa-
'cred Majesty, who, most unworthy, and ungar-
'nished by art or nature with rhetorical colours,
'have presumed to deliver your sacred Majesty,
'formed by nature, and framed by art and educa-
'tion to the perfection of all eloquence, the pub-
'lic message of your Majesty's loyal subjects here
'conveened, on the knees of my heart, beseech-
'ing your sacred Majesty, that my obedience to
'my superior's commands, may be a sacrifice ac-
'ceptable to expiate my presumption, your Ma-
'jesty's wonted clemency may give strength and
'vigour to my distrustful spirits, in gracious ac-
'ceptance of that which shall be delivered, and
'pardon my escapes. Receive then, dread Sove-
'reign, from your Majesty's faithful and loy-
'al subjects the magistrates and citizens of your
'highness's good town of Edinburgh, such wel-
'come as is due from these, who, with thankful
'hearts, do acknowledge the infinite blessings
'plenteously flowing to them from the paradise of
'your Majesty's unspotted goodness and virtue,
wishing your Majesty's eyes might pierce into
'their very hearts, to behold the excessive joy in-

' wardly conceived of the firſt meſſenger. Your
' Majeſty's princely reſolution to viſit your Majeſ-
' ty's good town, encreaſed by your Majeſty's coun-
' tenance, in proſecuting what was ſo happily in-
' tended, and new accompliſhed by your Majeſty's
' fortunate and ſafe return, which no tongue, how
' liberal ſoever, is capable to expreſs. Who ſhall
' conſider with an impartial eye, the continual
' carefulneſs your Majeſty had over us from your
' tender years, the ſettled temper of your Majeſty's
' government, wherein the niceſt eye could find
' no ſpot; yourſelf, as the life of the country, the
' father of the people, inſtructing not ſo much by
' precept, as example; your Majeſty's court the
' marriage place of wiſdom and godlineſs with-
' out impiety, cannot refuſe to avouch: But as
' your prudence has won the prize from all Kings
' and Emperors, that ſtand in the degree of com-
' pariſon; ſo hath your Majeſty's government
' been ſuch, that every man's eye may be a meſ-
' ſenger to his mind, that your Majeſty ſtands the
' quinteſſence of ruling ſkill of all proſperous and
' peaceable government, much wiſhed by our fore-
' fathers, but moſt abundantly enjoyed by us,
' praiſed be GOD, under your ſacred Majeſty.
' For if we ſhall, in a view, lay before us the
' times bypaſt, even ſince the firſt foundation of
' the kingdom, and therein conſider your Majeſ-
' ty's moſt noble progenitors, they were indeed all

'princes renowned for their virtues, not inferior
'to any Kings or Emperors of their time, they
'maintained and delivered their virgin fcepters
'unconquered, from age to age, from the foun-
'dation of the moft violent floods of conquering
'fwords, which overwhelmed the reft of the whole
'earth, and carried the crowns of all other Kings
'of this terreftrial ball unto thraldom; but far
'fhort of your Majefty's nature, having placed in
'your facred perfon alone, what in every one of
'them was excellent, the fenate houfe of the pla-
'nets being, as it were conveened at your Majef-
'ty's birth, for decreeing of all perfctions in your
'royal perfon, the heavens and earth witneffing
'your heroical frame, no influence whatfoever
'being able to bring the fame to a higher degree.
'If we fhall bring to mind the tumultuous days
'of your Majefty's more tender years, and there-
'in your Majefty's prudence, wifdom and con-
'ftancy, in uniting the disjointed members of the
'common wealth, who will not, with the Queen
'of Sheba, confefs he has feen more wifdom in
'your royal perfon, than report hath brought to
'foreign ears; and there is not of any eftate or
'age within this kingdom, who has not had parti-
'cular experience of the fame, and fenfibly felt
'the fruits thereof, the fire of civil difcord, which,
'as a flame, devoured us, was thereby quenched,
'every man poffeffed his own in peace, reaping

'that which he had sown, and enjoying the fruits
'of his own labours, your Majesty's great vigi-
'lance and godly zeal in propagating the gospel,
'and defacing the monuments of idolatry, banish-
'ing that Roman antichristian hierarchy, and
'establishing our church, repairing the ruins
'thereof, protecting us from foreign invasions,
'the rich trophies of your Majesty's victories
'more powerfully atchieved by your sacred wis-
'dom, deserves more worthily than those of the
'Cæsars, so much extolled by the ancients. All
'ages shall record, and posterity bless Almighty
'God, for giving us their fore-fathers a King, in
'heart upright as David, wise as Solomon, and
'godly as Josias.

'And who can better witness your Majesty's
'royal favour and beneficence, than this your
'good town of Edinburgh, which being founded
'in the days of that worthy King Fergus I. the
'first builder of the kingdom, and famous for her
'unspotted fidelity to your Majesty's most noble
'progenitors, was by them enriched with many
'freedoms, priviledges and dignities; all which
'your Majesty not only confirmed, but also, with
'accession of many more enlarged; beautified her
'with a new erected college, famous for profes-
'sion of all liberal sciences, so that she justly
'doth acknowledge your Maj^{n}y the author and

' conserver of her peace, her sacred physician,
' who binds up the wounds of her distracted com-
' mon wealth, the only *magnes* of her prosperity,
' and the true fountain, from whence under GOD,
' all her happiness and felicity floweth, and doth
' in all humility record your Majesty's royal favour
' extended to her at all times.

' NEITHER hath the ocean of your Majesty's
' virtues contained itself within the precinct of this
' isle; What ear is so barbarous, that hath not
' heard of the fame of your Majesty? What fo-
' reign prince is not indebted to your sacred wis-
' dom? What reformed church doth not bless
' your Majesty's birth day, is it not protected un-
' der the wings of your sacred authority, from anti-
' christian locusts, whose walls, by the sacred wis-
' dom wherewith your sacred person is endowed,
' hath been battered and shaken more, than did
' the Goths and Vandals the old frame of the
' same, by the sword: And for your sacred virtue,
' your Majesty deserves to be Monarch of the
' world: So for your piety and unfeigned zeal, in
' propagating and maintaining the gospel, does,
' of due, appertain to your Majesty, the titles of
' most Christian and Catholic King.

' FOR all which, your Majesty's most royal fa-
' vours, having nothing to render, but that which

' is due, we your Majesty's most humble subjects,
' prostrate at your sacred feet, lay down our lives,
' goods, liberties, and every thing that is dear to
' us, vowing to keep to your sacred Majesty, un-
' spotted loyalty and subjection, and ever to be
' ready to consecrate and sacrifice ourselves for
' maintainance of your royal person and estate,
' praying to the eternal, our GOD, that peace
' may be within your Majesty's walls, and prospe-
' rity within your palaces, length of days to your
' sacred person; that from your Majesty's loins
' may never be wanting one to sway the scenter of
' these your kingdoms, and that mercy may be to
' yourself and your seed for ever.

AFTER the delivery of this speech, his Majesty went to the great church; and there having heard sermon from the archbishop of St. Andrews, primate of all Scotland, proceeded on his march to his palace of Holy-rood-house; at the gate of the inner court was presented to his royal hands, a book in manuscript, of curious and learned verses in Greek and Latin, entitled, *Acadamiæ Edinburgensis Congratulatio*, and a speech made in name of that university by Mr. Patrick Nisbet. Next day, his Majesty was pleased to honour the university with his presence at a philosophical disputation in the oriental languages, by the professors of philosophy, Mr. John Adamson, Mr. James Fairly,

Mr. Patrick Sands, Mr. Andrew Young, Mr. James Reid, and Mr. William King. When the exercise was over, his Majesty was pleased to compliment the disputants in the following poem, which by them was variously pain Latin.

As Adam *was the first of men, whence all beginning take ;*
So Adam-son *was president, an l first man of this act.*
The Thesis Fair-lie *did defend, which tho' they lies contain ;*
Yet were fair Lies, and he the same right fairly did maintain.
The field first entered Mr. Sands, *and there he made me see,*
That not all Sands are barren Sands, but that some fertile be.
Then Mr. Young *most subtily the Thesis did impugn.*
And kythed old in Aristotle, *altho' his name be* Young.
To him succeeded Mr. Reid, *who tho' Red be his name,*
Need neither for his dispute blush, nor of his speech think shame.
Last enter'd Mr. King *the lists, and dispute like a King,*
How reason reigning like a Queen, should anger under-bring.

*To their deserved praise have I thus play'd upon
    their names,
And wills this College hence be call'd the College of
    King* JAMES.

MANIFOLD honours the King put upon this his good town of Edinburgh, in the castle whereof he was born; as appears by the inscription yet remaining in the room, where his mother queen Mary was delivered of him, which runs thus.

O JESU LORD, *who crownit was with thorn,
Preserve the birth whais badgie here is born,
And giant, O* LORD, *that whatever of her
    proceed,
May be unto thy honor and Glory. Soe beid.*

His Majesty by a charter under his great seal dispones to the provost, bailies, town council, and community of the burgh of Edinburgh, the jurisdiction, haven and harbour of Leith, and makes and constitutes them judges amongst the skippers, masters and mariners in Leith, and all other skippers, masters and sailors, as well his subjects, as foreigners, being for the time with their ships, boats, or barks within the same village of Leith, and harbour of the same, in all sea fareing actions and causes whatsomever, with power to them, to make acts and statutes, for the increase of sailing.

And difpones to them the prime gilt to be uplifted for fuftaining of poor indigent fea men within the faid village of Leith, forth of the freight of every tun of goods, in manner fpecified in the faid charter, to be applied to the ufe of the faid poor. This charter is dated at Whitehall 3d April 1616.

By another charter under the great feal, he confirms to the magiftrates, town-council, crafts, and community of the faid burgh, and their fucceffors, all former inffeoffments granted to them by his predeceffors, of the heretable offices of fheriff fhip, crownry, which contains a new gift of the fheriff-fhip and crownry within the faid burgh, common mills thereof, common muir, marifh, loch, part, ftreets, common ways, paffages and lonnings leading to and from the fame; and efpecially the paffage leading to Leith upon both fides of the water thereof, and to the faid village of Leith, haven of the famen, and within the harbour and village of Newhaven, and village of Leith, havens, roads, harbours and bulwarks thereof, and within the lands of common clofets, burfhoilf, paffages, and other bounds whatfoever, lying within the liberty of the faid burgh of Edinburgh. Dated at Whitehall, 3d April 616.

By another gift under his great feal, grants to

the said provost, bailies and council, the power of having the sword carried before them, riding of the marches or bounds thereof, and of the office of justice of peace, in manner therein contained. Dated at Whitehall, 10th November 1609.

By another gift, he enlarges their powers and justices of peace, in which they are inffeofft. Dated at Hamptoun Court, 25th September 1612.

By another gift and inffeoffment, grants to them all fines and ammerciaments, belonging to the office of sheriff-ship and justiciaries of peace. Dated at Whitehall, 17th September 1613.

By another charter under the great seal, dispones to them the custom or excise (and to their successors) of four pounds Scots, forth of every tun of wine to be retailed and vented in smalls within the said burgh, liberties and jurisdiction of the same, to be uplifted by their treasurers, collectors, and others in their names, from the retailers, vintners, tapsters, and sellers of the same, in all time coming. Dated at Whitehall, 10th November 1609.

By a ratification of the said gift, and new disposition, he dispones the foresaid custom and excise of four pound, forth of every tun retailed within the said burgh, and within the village of Leith, in all parts within the same upon the south-side of the water of Leith. Dated at Hamptoun, 25th September 16 2.

By another under the great seal, power to them and their successors, to erect a weigh-house at the Over-tron of the said burgh, with divers liberties, duties, and immunities therein contained. Dated at Royston, 9th December 1611.

By a charter under his great seal, dispones that part of the lands of Highrigs, containing 10 acres of land or thereby. Dated at Edinburgh, 30th July 1618..

By a gift under his great seal, gives and grants the Jedgry of Salmon, herring, and white fish, packed and peilled within the kingdom of Scotland. Dated at Royston, 19th October 1618.

By another gift under his great seal, the power of being overseers and visiters of all measurers and sellers of cloath, stuffs, and stockings, made in the said village of Leith and sherifidom of Edinburgh. Dated at Whitehall, 8th March 1621.

By a charter under his great seal, dated at Stirling, 14th April 1582, ratifying a charter made by Queen Mary under her great seal. Dated 13th March 1566, of the lands, tenements, houses and biggings, churches, chaplainries, altarages and prebendaries in whatsoever churches, chaples or colleges, within the liberty of the said burgh, founded by whatsoever person, whereof the saids chaplains and prebends were in possession, with the yards, orchards, annualrents, teinds, services, profits, duties, emoluments which pertained thereto and of all lands which pertained to the black friars and gray friars.

By another charter, he ratifies and approves the demission and ratification made by John Gib, in favours of the said burgh, of the provostry of the Kirkfield, haill lands and biggings belonging to the same. And dispones the liberty of a college, and repairing sufficient houses for accommodating the professors of philosophy, humanity and languages, theology, medicine, law, and all other sciences; and electing sufficient professors for teaching the said professions; and for that effect, disponed to them the provostry of Kirkfield, with the tenements, fruits, possessions, rents and duties thereof.

By another charter under his great seal, 4th April 1584, considering, That the burgh of Edinburgh had been at great expences in erecting the said college, and had gifted great sums for sustaining the professors, for instructing the youth, he disponed to the good town, for the use of the said college, and for maintainance of the principal and regents, the arch-deanry of Lothian, containing the parsonage of Curry, with the manse, glebe and kirk lands, teinds and duties of the same.

By another charter under his great seal, 26th May 1587, for the great expences wared out by the good town, in erecting an hospital for maintaining their ministers, disponed to the town the provostry of the Trinity college. house-rents, kirk-teinds, and fruits thereto pertaining.

By another charter under his great seal, 29th July 1587, ratifies the inffeoffments granted by himself and Queen Mary his mother, of the said Kirk-lands, Trinity college, provostry of Kirkfield, and arch-deanry of Lothian, for the use of the ministers, college, and poor.

By another charter under the great seal, dated at Bearboar castle, 1612, ratifies all former grants of the said Kirk lands, provostries of Kirkfield, and Trinity-college, and arch-deanry of Lothian, with a new gift of the saids haill Kirk lands for maintaining the ministers, college and poor.

Thus did that just and gracious prince show his beneficence to our metropolis, as the wise King Solomon, in his book of Ethicks, remarks, *When the righteous are in authority the city rejoiceth; but when the wicked bear rule, the people mourn.* And being a peaceful prince as well as generous, he poured oil into the wounds of his people, and healed the growing contentions betwixt the merchants and trades, by the subsequent decreet-arbitral.

At Halyraidhouse, the twenty twa day of Apryl, the yeir of God one thousand five hundred four score three years; we Robert Fairlie of Braid, Sir Archibald Naper of Edinbellie knight, and James Johnstoun of Elphingstoun, Judges Arbitrators, chosen for the part of Mr. Michael Chisholme, Andrew Sclater, John Adamsone, and William Fairlie bailies of Edinburgh, Mr. John Prestoun dean of gild, Mungo Russel treasurer, John Johnstoun, Robert Ker younger, Henry Charters, John Morisone, William Maul, John Harwood, John Robertsone, William Inglis, Alexander Naper, William Nesbet merchants; being on the counsel of the said burgh, for themselves, and in name and behalf, and as commissioners for the haill merchants indwellers of the said burgh, on the ane part, and John Cockburn of Ormestoun, Mr Robert Pont provost of the Trinity-colledge, and Mr. David Lindsey minister of Leith, judges arbitrators chosen for the part of James Fergusone bower, John Bairnsfather tailyeour, twa of the crafts-men, being on the counsel of the said burgh; Gilbert Prymrose deaken of the chirurgians, John Watt deaken of the hammermen, William Hoppringle deaken of the tailyeours, Edward Galbraith deaken of the skinners, Edward Hant deaken of the goldsmiths, Adam Newtown deaken of the baxters, Thomas Dicksone deaken of the furriers, Andrew Williamsone deaken of the Wrights, William Bickertoun deaken of the maissons, James Ker, deaken of the fleshers, William Weir deaken of the cordiners, Thomas Wright deaken of the websters, William Cowtts deaken of the wakers, and William Somer deaken of the bonnetmakers; for themselves, and in name and behalf, and as commissioners for the haill crafts-men, indwellers of the said brugh, on the uther part: And the right potent and illuster prince, JAMES be the grace of GOD, King of Scots, our Soveraign Lord, ods man and overs man, commonly chosen by advice and consent of baith the saids parties, anent the removing of all questions, differences and controversies, quhilks are, or hes been betwixt the saids merchants, concerning whatsomever cause or occasion whereupon debate or question did arise in any time betwixt them. And thereupon, baith the saids parties being bund, oblist, and sworn, to stand, abide, underly, and fulfil the decreet-arbitral, and deliverance of us the saids judges and overs-man, but appellation, reclamation, or contradiction, as at length is contained in ane submission made thereupon, baith the saids parties clames and griefs given in be them, with the answers made thereto, and their rights, reasons, and alledgances being heard, seen, and considered be us, and we therewith being ryply advysit, after many sundry conventions and meetings, with lang travels tane hereanent, hes all in ane voice accordit, decernit, and concludit, upon the heads and articles following.

FIRST, To take away all differences quhilk hes been heretofore, concerning the persons who had the government of the town, their number, power, or authority, and manner of their election; it is finally accordit and decernit thereupon as follows:

MAGISTRATS.

THE magistrats, sic as provest, bailies, dean of gild, and thesaurer, to be in all tymes coming of the estait and calling of merchants, conforme to the acts of parliament; and if any crafts-man exerceand merchandize, sall for his guid qualities be promovit theirto, in that caise he sall leive his craft, and not occupy the fame be himfelf nor his fervants during the tyme of his office, and fall not return theirto at any tyme theireafter, quhill he obtein fpecial licence of the proveft, bailies and counfel to that effect.

Counsel.

THE counfel to confift of ten merchants, to wit, The auld proveft, four auld bailies, dean of gild and thefaurer of the nixt year preceeding, and three merchants to be chofen to them, and als to confift of eight crafts-men theirof, fex deakens, and twa uther crafts men, makand in the haill the faid counfel eighteen perfons, and this by the office men of that year, to wit, the proveft, bailies, dean of gild, and thefaurer.

Election.

AND as to the manner of their election, it is firft generally accordit and agriet, that na manner of perfon be chofen proveft, bailies, dean of gild, or thefaurer, fuppofe they be burgeffes of the burgh, and able therefore, without they have been ane year or twa upon the counfel of before. And anent the counfel, the auld manner of giving in of tickets be the deakens, out of the quhilk the twa crafts men were yearly chofen to be abrogat, ceafe and expyre in all tymes coming, swa that the saids twa crafts men shall be chosen yearly without any ingiving of tickets indifferently, of the best and worthiest of the crafts, be the saids provest, bailies, dean of gild, thesaurer and counsel alanerly, and nane to be on the counsel above twa year together, except they be office-men, or be vertue of their offices be on the counsel. Sicklike, anent the lytts to be bailies, they sall not be dividet nor casten in four ranks, three to every rank, as they were wont to be; bot to be chosen indifferently, ane out of the twelff lytts, the third out of ten, and the fourt out of nyne lytts. Anent the deakens, that nane be electit deaken, except he that hes been an maister of his craft twa year at the least; and that nane of them be continued in their offices of deakenship above twa year togidder. Last in general, that nane have vote in lytting, voiting, electing of the provest, bailies, counsel, deakens, dean of gild, or thesaurer, but the persons hereafter following, in maneer after-specifiet.

Election in special of DEAKENS.

AND to proceid to the said election: It is found guid to begin at the choosing of the deakens of crafts, quhilks are fourteen in number, to wit, chirurgeons, goldsmyths, skinners, furriers, hammermen, wrights, masons, tailyeours, baxters, fleshers, cordiners, websters, wakers, bonnetmakers; swa the deakens now present shall stand and continue quhil the third counsel-day of before the auld time of election of the new counsel, quhilk was on the Wednesday next preceeding the feast of Michaelmass; upon the quhilk third counsel-day, the provest, bailies, and counsel now stand, and, extending to nineteen persons, and fra thence furth yearly, and ilk year, the provest, bailies and counsel, constitute of the said twenty five persons, sall call in before them the saids deakens of crafts, every ane severally, and inquire their opinion and judgement of the best and worthiest of their crafts, thereafter, the saids provest, bailies and counsel, shall nominate and lytt three persons of the maist discreet, godly, and qualified persons of every ane of the saids fourteen crafts, maist expert hand-labourers of their awen craft, burgesses and freemen of the burgh of Edinburgh, whereof the auld deaken shall be ane, and cause deliver their names to the deakens, every ane according to their craft. Quhilk deakens, on the morn thereafter, sall assemble and convein their crafts, and every craft be themselves, furth of thir names shall elect ane person wha sall be their deaken for that year, and upon the next counsel day after the said election, the auld deakens, with some of the masters of their crafts, fall present the new deakens to the counsel, quha fall authorize them in their offices.

New Counsel of DEAKENS.

NEXT, to proceed to the election of the new counsel. The said day of presenting of the new deakens, the provest, bailies, and counsel now standand of nineteen persons, and fra then furth, the said day yearly; the provest, bailies and counsel, of twenty five persons, fall choose furth of the saids fourteen deakens, sex persons to be adjoined with the new counsel for the year to come, and to have special vote in lytting and choosing of the provest, bailies and counsel; and the same day, the auld sex deakens quhilk was upon the counsel the year preceeding, to be removed, and have na farther vote for that year, except some of them be of the number of the new elected deakens.

New Counsel of MERCHANTS and CRAFTS.

THEREAFTER, Upon the Wednesday next, preceeding Michaelmass ilk year, the provest, bailies, dean of gild, thesaurer, and ten merchants of the counsel, and the said sex deakens, and twa crafts-men, and in the haill twenty five persons, and twenty sex votes, be reason of the provest's twa votes ordinarly standand at all tymes, fall conveen and choofe the new counfel, to the number of eighteen perfons, to wit, the auld proveft, bailies, dean of gild and thefaurer of that year, and the faid fex deakons, to make thirteen perfons thereof, and to them to be chofen three merchants, and twa crafts men, and thir perfons to be callit the new counfel, and if any perfon of the merchants chofen upon the counfel, happens to be put on the lytte of ane uther office, and promovit thereto, an uther fall be chofen in his room be the faids proveft, bailies and counfel.

Lytts of MAGISTRATS.

THIRDLY, To proceid to the choofing of the lytts to the magiftrats and office men, fic as proveft, bailies, dean of gild and thefaurer, upon the Friday nixt thereafter, there fall conveen the faid new counfel of eighteen perfons, and the auld counfel conftitute of twelff perfons, viz. ten merchants, and twa crafts-men, and in the haill thretty perfon's to the proveft's odd vote; quhilks perfons fo folemnatly protefting before GOD, that they fhall choofe the perfons whom they find maift meet, without favour, hatred, or any kind of collufion; then fall begin and choofe the lytts to the faid magiftrats and office-men, to every ane of them three lytts; that is to fay, to the proveft, twa lytts with himself; to the four bailies, every ane of them three lytts, the auld bailies not beand ane, except they be new chosen thereto; to the dean of gild, twa lytts with himself; and to the thesaurer, twa lytts with himself: Quhilk haill lytts be of the order and calling of merchants, as said is.

Election of MAGISTRATS.

FOURTHLY, To proceed to the electing and choosing of the said magistrats and office-men; upon the Tuesday nixt after Michaelmas yearly, there sall conveen the saids thretty persons, of new and auld counsel, and with them the rest of the deakens of crafts quhilks are not of the counsel, extending to eight persons; the haill person swa conveenand, extending to thretty eight persons by the provost's odde vote, whereof twenty merchants, and eighteen crafts-men; quhilks persons sall begin at the lytts of the provest, and every ane in their awen rank, give their votes to sic as they find meet for the weill of the town, according to their conscience and knawledge, but feid or favour; and on whom greatest number of votes sall fall, that he be sworn, receivit and admitit provest for that year; and swa to proceed thorow the lytts of the bailies, dean of gild and thesaurer, quhill the saids election be compleatly endit. The saids provest, bailies, dean of gild, thesaurer and coun-

sel, electit, as said is, makand in the haill twenty
five persons; they only, and nae uthers, sall have
the full government and administration of the hail
common-weal of this burgh, in all things, as the
proveſt, bailies, and counsel thereof, or of any
uther brugh had of before, or may have hereafter,
be the laws or consuetude of this realm, infeoffments and priviledges grantit to this town be our
Sovereign Lord's maiſt noble progenitors, except-
and always thir causes following, in the quhilks
the hail fourteen deakens of crafts sall be callit and
adjoined with them, to give their special vote and
consultation thereinto, to wit, in election of the
proveſt, bailies, dean of gild and thesaurer, as said
is, in setting of fews, or any manner of tacks, attour the yearly rowping, on Martinmass even, in
giving of benefices, and uther offices in brugh, in
granting of extents, contributions, emprimits,
and sicklike bigging of common warks, and in
disponing of the common-good, above the sum of
twenty pound togidder.

Wairning of the DEAKENS and COUNSEL.

PROVIDING nevertheless, that the deakens
not of the counsel, or any of them, beand person-
ally warned to that effect, and absenting themselfs,

fwa oft the laft deakens, or any uther that was in lytt with him that yeir, fhall fupplie their room; and they beand perfonally warned, and abfent, the reft compearand fall have power to proceed. If any of the proveft, baillies, and counfel be abfent, the reft wha are prefent fall choofe an other in their room. And to avoid all fufpicion that hes rifen in times paft, through the particular affemblies and conventions, contrair to the acts of parliament, and to the trouble of the quyet eftait of this brugh.

CONVENTIOUNS.

IT is agriet and conludit, that nather the merchants amang themfelfs, nather the crafts and their deakens or vifitors, fall have, or make any particular, or general conventions, as deaken with deakens, deakens with their crafts, or crafts amang themfelfs, far lefs to make privat laws, or ftatutes, poynd and diftrenzie at their awen hands for tranfgreffions, by the advice and confent of the proveft, bailies and counfel.

DEAN of GILD may convœen his COUNSEL.

EXCEPTAND always, that the dean of gild may affemble his brethern and council in their gild courts, conform to their ancient lawes of the gildrie, and priviledges thereof: And that any ane craft may conveen together amang themſelfs, for the chooſing of their deakens at the tyme appointit thereto, and in manner before expreſt; making of maſters, and trying of their handie-wark allanerly. And if any brethren, or deakens of crafts, ſall find out, or devyſe any good heids, that may tend to the weill of their craft, they ſall propone the ſame to the magiſtrates, wha ſall ſet forward an act or ſtatute thairupon.

COMMISSIONERS.

ITEM, As tuitching the commiſſioners in parliament, general counſel, and commiſſioners in conventioun of burrows, it is though guid be the commiſſioners, that in all tyms coming be ane of the ſaids commiſſioners for the brugh of Edinburgh, ſall be choſen be the ſaid proveſt and bailies, furth of the number and calling of the crafts-men, and that perſon to be ane burgeſs and gild brother of the brugh, of the beſt, expert and wiſe, and of honeſt converſation.

AUDITORS.

ITEM, It is agreed, that the auditors of all the towns compts ſall hereafter be choſen of equal number of merchants and crafts-ment be the proveſt, bailies, and counſel.

GILDRIE.

ITEM, Toward the lang controverſies for the gildrie, it is finally with common conſent, appointit, agriet and concludit, that als weill craftsmen, as merchants, ſall be received and admitted gild brether, and the ane not to be refuſit, or ſecludit therefrae mair nor the uther, they being burgeſſes of the burgh, als meit and qualified thairfore; and that gild-brether have liberty to uſe merchandice. their admiſſion, and tryal of their qualificatioun, to be in the power and hands of the proveſt, bailies, theſaurer, and counſel, with the dean of gild, and his counſel, quhilk ſall conſiſt in equal number of merchants and crafts-men, gild brether, not exceiding the number of ſex perſons, by the dean of gild himſelf; and that no perſon, of what faculty ſoever he be, ſall bruik the benefit of an gild brother, without he be receivit and admittit thereto, as ſaid is.

BURGESSES, CRAFTS.

ITEM, That na manner of perſon be ſufferit to uſe merchandice, or occupy the handie wark of ane free crafts-man within this brugh, or yet to exerce the liberty and priviledge of the said burgh, without he be burgess and free-man of the same.

Extents.

ITEM, Becaufe the merchants and crafts-men of this burgh, are now to be incorporate in ane fociety, and to make an haill town, and an commod-weill, it is thought guid and expedient, and concludit, to abrogat the former cuftome of dividing and fetting of extents, wherein the merchants payit four pairts, and the crafts the fift part. And therefore it is agried, that as they watch and waird together: Swa in all extents, emprimits, contributions, and the like fubfidies to be impofit upon the brugh, merchants and crafts-men to bear the burden and charge thereof indifferently overheld, according to their ability and fubftance, throw the haill quarters of the town, without divifion of the rolls in merchants and crafts-men in any tyme coming; the extentours fall be of equal number of merchants and crafts-men, eight perfons of the ane calling, and eight perfons of the uther, to be electit, fworn and receivit be the proveft, bailies, and counfel, out of the maift difcreit and fkilful of all the town, void of all partial affectioun and hatred: And that na perfon ufand the trade of merchant or crafts man, and occupy and the friedome of the brugh, and able to pay any extent, not beirand the office of provest or bailies in the mean time, sall be any wayis exemit frae the real and actual payment thereof.

COLLECTIOUN.

ITEM, As the haill body of the town, consistand of merchants and crafts-men, does beir an common burden of watching, wairding, extenting, and of the like public charges, having an commoun good proper to nane, swa neidful it is for making an equal unity, and charitable concord, that there be in the hail town but an collection, and an purse, not peculiar to any, bot common to all, of the haill duties and casualities, callit the entres silver of prenteisses, up-setts, owkly pennies, unlaws, and sicklike, to be collectit in all tyme coming, and received baith of merchants and crafts-men, and put in an common purse, and to that effect the merchants to take and have prentices, als weill as crafts-men, and to be astrictit and obliest theirto, and na prentice alwayes to be received of ather of them, for shorter tyme nor the space of fyve yeirs compleit. And for the better knowledge to be had heirof, and for observin gan good ordour in collectioun of the same, that there be an commoun book made, keipit be the commoun clerk of this brugh present, and to come, wherein the names of all prentices to merchants and craftsmen, the name of their master, day of their entreis, and space of their prentiship, sall be insert and buikit: For the quhilk, the clerk sall have at their buiking of ilk person, sex pennies, and for the out-draught twelff pennies, quhilk buik sall be to the prentice an sufficient probatioun of his entres, and an charge to the collectors of the said dewties. If any man be an prentice an heireafter, and not put in the said buik, his prenteiship sall be to him of na effect. Alswa, be reason every industry is not of like valour and substance, it is declarit what ilk rank or degree of prentiesses sall pay; to wit, the merchant prenties, and sic kind of people as were wont to extent with them, and are not under an of the said fourteen carfts, to pay at his entres the day of his buiking, to the said collectioun thirtie shilling, and at his up-sett, or end of his prenteiship fyve pund The prenteis to an skinner, chirugean, goldsmyth, flesher, cordiner, tailyeour, baxter, and hammermen, at their entry and buiking, to the said collectioun twenty shilling, and for their up-sett fyve pund: The prenteis to an masoun and wrigh, at his entrie threteen shilling four pennies, and his up sett, three pund sex shilling eight pennies. The prenteis to an webster, waker, bonnetmaker, furrier, at his entry, ten shilling, and for his up-sett fyftie shilling; and thir dewties to be tane by their owkly pennies, and dewties of their burge-ſhips. And to cauſe all perſons to be mair willing to enter themſelfs in prenteiſhip with the burgeſſes and friemen of the brugh, this priviledge is grantit to the ſaids prenteiſes, that they ſall pay nae mair for their burgeſhip to the dean of gild, but fyve punds by the dewties foirſaids. And in augmentatioun of the ſaid collectioun, when any perſon ſall happen to be made burgeſſ.s of this brugh, wha was na prenteis to an merchant, or crafts man, frie burgeſs of the ſaid brugh, or hes not compleit his prenteiſhip, ſall pay to the ſaid collectioun at his admiſſioun, the double of the haill prentecis or entres-ſilver, up ſett and buiking, by the dewty payit to the dean of gild for his burgeſhip, or gildrie, quhilk is twenty punds for his burgeſhip, and fourty pound for his gildrie, the priviledge always of the bairns of burgeſſes and gild brether not being prejudged heirby, quha ſall pay the auld and accuſtomed dewty to the dean of gild allanerly. Thir dewties and collectiouns, or caſualities of entres-ſilver, up ſetts, owkly pennies, un laws, and ſik-like, to be received in all tyme coming, of all merchants and crafts-men indifferently, put in the ſaid common purſe, and imploit be the advice and command of the proveſt, bailies and counſel, for ſupport and relief of the failyiet and decayet burgeſſes and crafts men, their wyfes, bairns, and auld ſervants, and uther poor indwellers of the town. The proveſt, bailies, counſel, and haill deakens every yeir after electioun of the magiſtrates, ſall chooſe the collectors of the ſaid dewties and caſualities, of equal number of merchants and craftſmen, and to devyſe and ſet down ſic good ordour as they ſall find meet and expedient for the perfyte and readie in-bringing thereof. And laſt, the ſaid collectors ſall make yeirly compts of their intromiſſioun therewith, at the tyme of making of the town's compts, and ſall find ſufficient caution at their admiſſioun, for compts, reckoning and payment. *Item*, It is ordained, that baith the ſaids parties, merchants and craftſmen now preſent, and their ſucceſſors, ſall inviolably obſerve, keip, and fulfill this preſent appointment and decreit arbitral, and every heid, clauſe, and article conteinit therein. Likeas, his Majeſty, and the ſaids judges, wills and ordains them, with willing hearts, to put in oblivion all bypaſt enormities, imbrace and intertein love and amity, and as they are of ane city, ſwa to be of ane mind; then ſall they be acceptit of God, ſtop the mouths of them quhilk tuik occaſion be their diviſion to ſlander the truth; then ſall they be mair able to do our Soveraign Lord acceptable ſervice, and have ane ſtanding and flouriſhing commonweall. And finally, his Majeſty and the ſaids judges will eſteem their lang travels fruitfully beſtowit.

CERTIFICATION *of the* SETT.

ATTOUR, his Majesty and the saids judges, ordains the practice and execution of this present appointment and decreet to be and begin after the day and date hereof, and to continue, and be observit and keipit as ane perpetual law in tyme coming; and whasoever contraveins the samen, sall be repute and halden ane troubler of the quiet estate of the common-weal, incurre the note of infamy, and forfault and tyne their freedom for ever, and otherways to be persewit and punishit as seditious persons, conform to the laws of the realm, with all rigour and extremity; and ordains thir presents to be ratifiet and approvit in his highness next parliament; and in the mean tyme the same to be actit and registrat in the buiks of counsel and session, and to have the strength of acts and decreets of the lords thereof, and that their authority be interponit thereto, and letters and executorials to pass thereupon, in form as effeirs; and for acting and registrating of the samen, makes and constituts, Messers John Sharp, John prestoun, Thomas Craig and John Skeen, our procurators, conjunctly and severally *in ubericri forma promittendo de rato.* In witness whereof, the saids judges and overseman togidder, with the saids commissioners, in token of their consents and acceptation of the premiflis, has fubfcrivit tbir prefents with their hands, day, year, and place forefaids.

JAMES R. &c.

ALL the charters and donations in favours of the town of Edinburgh, granted before and fince the union of the two crowns of Scotland and England, were confirmed by the fucceeding Monarch, CHARLES I.

WHOSE charter of confirmation narrates, ' That
' calling to his royal memory, and perfectly un-
' derftanding the many good, notable, and thankful
' fervices performed by the magiftrates and inha-
' bitants of Edinburgh, the chief city and burgh
' of the ancient kingdom of Scotland, not only
' to himfelf, fince his happy acceffion to the king-
' dom, but alfo to his deareft father of eternal
' memory, and his other moft famous progenitors,
' the particular and notable expreffions whereof,
' are contain'd in the ancient infeoffments granted
' to them by his predeceffors of eternal memory;
' which remains to pofterity, as figns of their fi-
' delity, and great and egregious fervices done,
' and performed by them, for the good and ho-
' nour of the kingdom: Therefore, confirmed,
' &c.' And did grant to the magiftrates of the faid town and fucceffors, the prefenting and nomi-

minating of ministers, for serving the cures in the haill churches built, or to be built, within the said town with the right of patronage of the said haill kirks in all time coming. As also, confirmed to them, the said city, town-walls, ditches, ports, streets, passages, paths, lands, teritories and community of the same, with the common lands, called, the Common Muir easter and wester, and common mire thereof; together with the south loch, called the Barron Loch, and the loch of the said city, called the North Loch, with the lands, of old called the Greenside, with the Leper-house and yard situate on the same, arable lands, banks and marishes thereof, for the present occupied by the lepers of the said house. And granted to the said burgh, the sole liberty of merchandize pertaining to a free royal burgh, within the bounds of the sheriffdom of Edinburgh, and the privileges of weekly markets every Monday, Wednesday and Friday, or any three days of the week that they shall appoint, with two yearly fairs, viz. Hallow-fair and Trinity-fair, with the haill small customs, according to use and wont, especially the sheriff fee and sheriff gloves. And thereby enacted the village of Leith into a burgh of barony, with power to the magistrates of Edinburgh, to choice bailies and officers therein, and making laws for governing thereof. Which charter is dated at Newmarket, 23d October 1636, and

12th year of his reign, before witnesses, the most reverend father in Christ, and his well-beloved Counsellor, John, by the mercy of GOD, Archbishop of St. Andrews, primate and metropolitan of the kingdom of Scotland, &c. his chancellor; his well beloved cousen and counsellor, James Marquis of Hamilton, earl of Arran Cambridge, Lord Aven and Innerdale, &c. Thomas Earl of Haddington, Lord Binning and Byris, keeper of the privy Seal; William Earl of Stirling, Viscount of Canada, Lord Alexander of Tullibody, &c. his secretary; his well-beloved familiar counsellor Sir John Hay of Barro, clerk to his council, registers, and rolls; John Hamilton of Orbistoun justice clerk; John Scot of Scotstarvit, director to our chancellary knights.

THESE charters shew the pious care and compassion of our sovereigns for the poor: And here, I were very unjust to our mother city, as well as to the memory of that great, good man, George Heriot, burgess and goldsmith of Edinburgh, jeweller to the two renowned princes, JAMES VI. and this king CHARLES; if I should forget his pious mortification to the poor, and the magnificent fabric which he erected for their hospital, Anno 1627. The mortifications I have formerly mentioned relating to St. Eloi and St. Mungo's altars, flowed rather from self interest than charity, the patrons believing, by their donations, to merit heaven, as the charters expresses it, (such is the blindness of popery) and claimed it as purchased and paid for: But this Protestant founder, was a stranger to the uncouth doctrine of merit; he knew, that salvation is the gift of GOD through CHRIST JESUS; That good works is the fruit and natural result of faith; that rich men are the stewards of GOD's goodness, the messengers of his favours, the conduit-pipes of his liberality; and therefore, in the statutes of the hospital, *Caput de fundatore hospitai,* statutes, that on the first Monday of June every year, thanks be given to GOD in the Grayfriar's church, for the charitable maintenance which the poor maintained in the hospital, receive by the bounty of the founder; and that the preacher exhort all men of ability to follow his example, to urge the necessity of good works for the testimony of their faith; and to clear the doctrine of the church from the reproaches of adversaries, who give us out to be the impugners of good works.

THE fundamental institutions of this hospital were, at the desire of the founder, compiled by the reverend doctor Walter Balcanquhall the dean of Rochester, who left considerably to it himself.

If God records Bezaleel and Aholiah, two goldsmiths and jewellers, Exod. xxxi. for their curious workmanship in the tabernacle, we ought certainly to record a goldsmith and jeweller, who not only excelled in architecture, sculpture, and engraving; but dedicated a palace, and prince's revenues to the Lord, Psal. cxii. 9. *He hath dispersed, he hath given to the poor, his righteousness endureth for ever, his horn shall be exalted with honour.*

The greatest part of this stately edifice is Gothick work; but the frontispiece is adorned with stately pillars of the Corinthian and Dorick order, with various groops of figures, two of which are very curious, a company of school boys, in the habits appointed by the founder, under the ferula of their preceptors, with this motto, extending to the face of the teachers, *Sic vos Deus, ut vos eos;* and the other, the scholars round the table at dinner, this inscription above their heads, out of the poet *Virgil, Deus nobis hæc otia fecit.* Above this, the arms of the founder; within the porch above the entry, in a nich, the statute of the partron, above his head this motto, alluding as well to the building, as to the builder: *Corporis hæc, Animi est hoc Opus Effigies.*

The entry of the chapel beautified with pillars

of the Teutonick order, and a large bible engraven in stone, above which is this inscription.

Aurifici dederat mihi vis divina perennem, & facere in Terris, in Cœlo & Ferre.

BELOW an artificial crown, which supplies the word *Coronam*, the sentence being designed for an Ænigma

I. The Royal College of SURGEONS

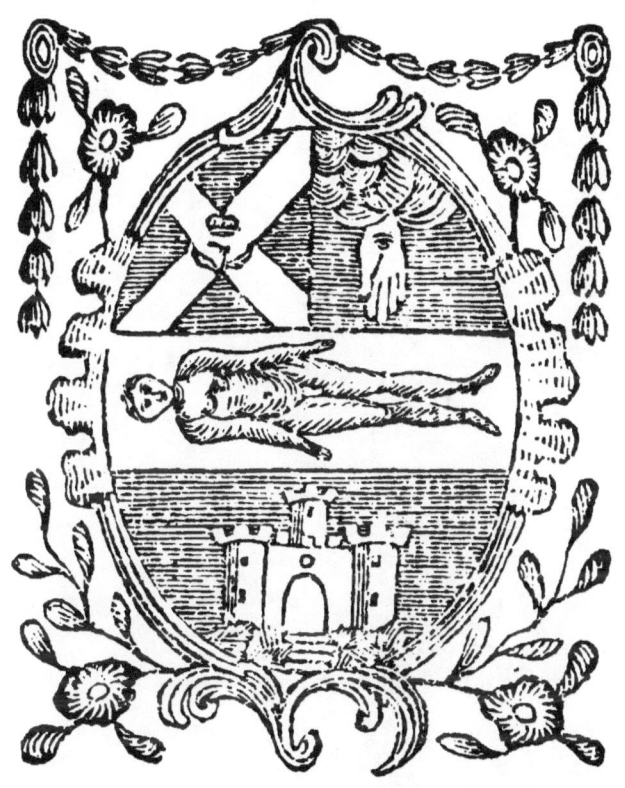

The Surgeons and Barbers were erected in to a corporation by a Seal of Cause, at Edinburgh, 1. July 1504, and ratified by King James the V. 13. October 1506, &c.

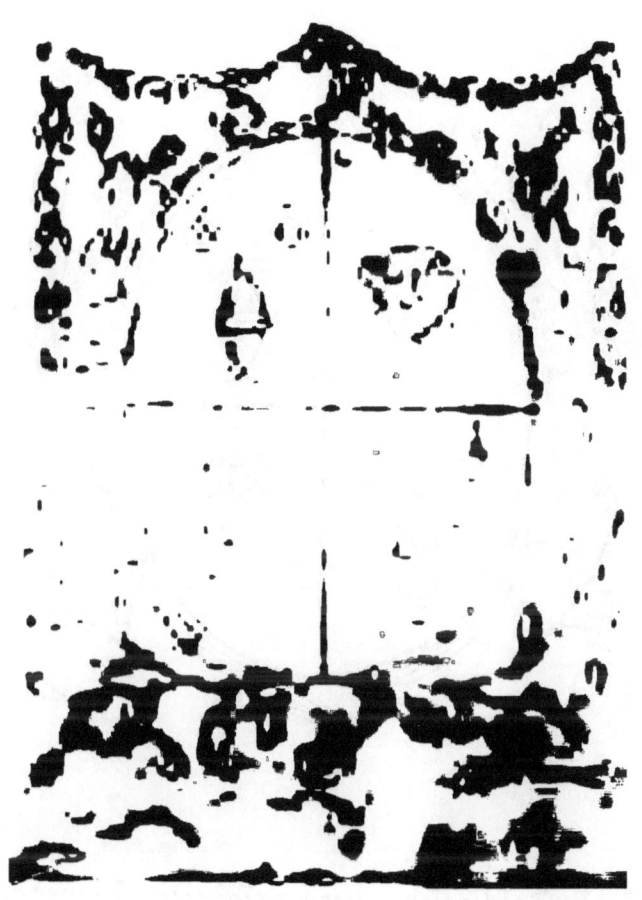

II, GOLDSMITHS.

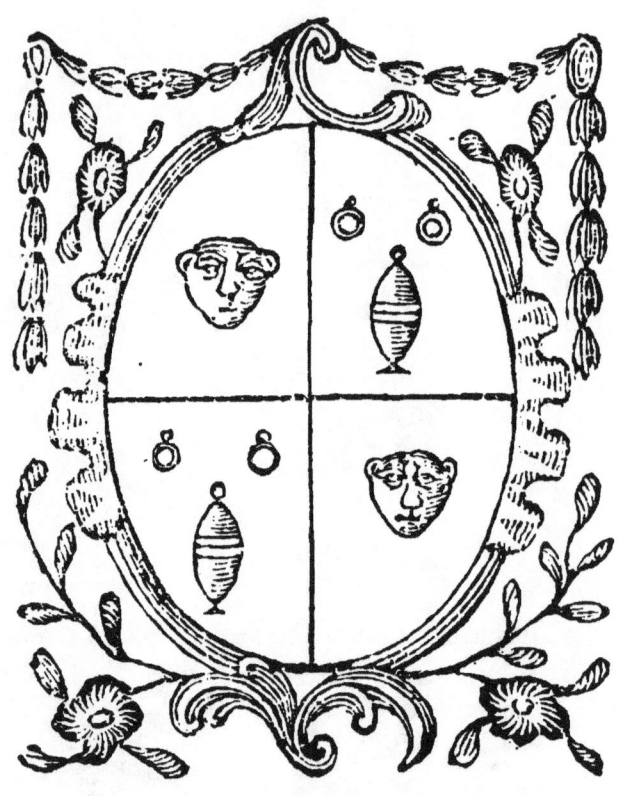

THE Goldsmiths were originally Incorporated with the Hammermen, but what time they seperat them is uncertain; they were, however, compa y in 1581.

III. Skinners.

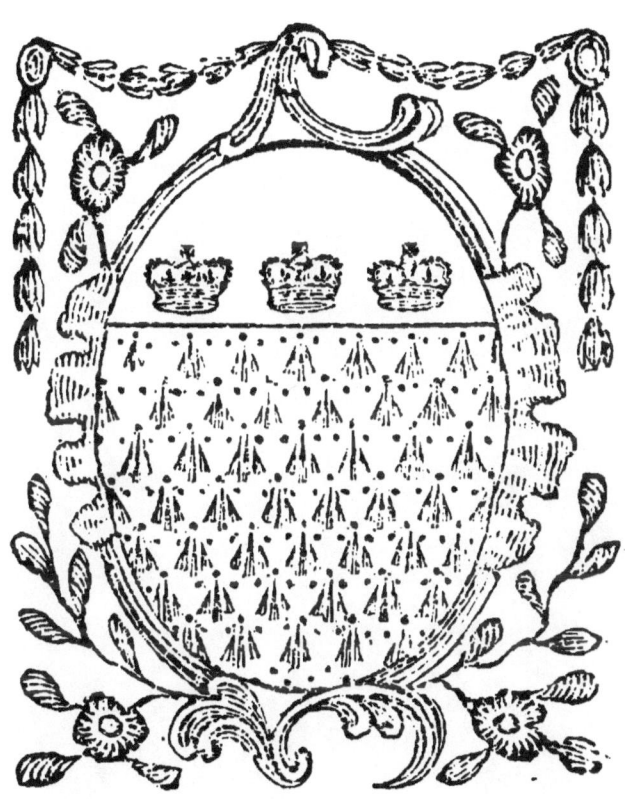

THE Skinners were erected into a corporation, on or before the year 1586.

IV. Furriers.

THE Furriers alfo owe their exiftance, as a body, corporate, to the Town council: The time of heir being incorporated is unknown.

V. HAMMERMENS.

THE Hammermen were erected into a corporation 2. May 1583. See the City Set.

VI. Wrights

THE Wrights have a double reprefentation in the Town-Council.

VII. Masons.

THE Masons and Wrights were Incorporated the 15. October 1475. See the City Set.

VIII. Tailors.

THE Tailors were Incorporated, and has several Charters from the Town Council, ratified by the Scots Kings.

IX. BAXTERS.

A SEAL of Cause from the Town Council in 1522, infavour of this Corporation; by this Charter they had an altar erected in St Giles's Church,

X. Fleshers.

THEY are an old Corporation, they were Incorporated before 1488, for in that year several regulations were made. See the City Set.

XI. CORDINERS.

WE cannot ascertain the time that this Corporation was instituted, Maitland places it in 1449; but the earliest records that can be recovered is 1475, ratified by King James VI.

XII. WEBSTERS.

THE Weavers were incorporated 31. January 1475. They petitioned, " That for the honour and love of God, of his Mother the Virgin, and of St. Sovrane"; and prays a ratification of these a ticles, among others, care is taken to enact " that the priest shall get his meat.

SET or CHARTER for the Government of the City of EDINBURGH.

Magistrates.

THE magistrates of the city of Edinburgh, to be seven in number, viz, a provost, four bailies, dean of guild, and treasurer; and these to be always of the estate and calling of merchants, conform to acts of parliament; and if any craftsman shall, for his good qualities, be promoted thereto, in that case he shall leave his craft, and not occupy the same by himself, or his servants, during the time of his office, and shall not return thereto at any time thereafter, until he obtain special licence from the provost, bailies, and council to that effect.

Town Council.

THE town council to consist of ten merchants, viz. the old provost, four old bailies, old dean of guild, and old treasurer, and three merchants to be added to these (called merchant counsellors), and also to consist of eight craftsmen, viz. six deacons, and two other craftsmen (called trades counsellors), making in all eighteen; and these, added to the magistrates for the year, form the ordinary council of twenty-five.

INCORPORATIONS.

THE fourteen incorporated trades, or crafts, are the surgeons, goldsmiths, skinners, furriers, hammermen, wrights, masons, tailors, baxters, fleshers, cordiners, websters, waulkers, and bonnetmakers *.

---

* The surgeons and barbers were formerly incorporated together; but some differences arising betwixt them, a long process at law ensued, the result of which was, the professions were disjoined, and the barbers are now only a society, though retaining the privileges granted by royal charter: they chuse a preses, instead of a deacon, and are not represented in the town-council.

The furriers are now known by the name of glovers.

Along with the hammermen are comprehended the following crafts viz. blacksmiths, white-ironsmiths, coppersmiths, locksmiths, sheersmiths, gunsmiths, cutlers, pewterers, saddlers, armourers, founders, braziers, watchmakers, hookmakers, pinmakers, and beltmakers.

The wrights and masons are known by the name of " the united incorporation of Mary's chapel."—It consists of the following crafts, viz. wrights, masons, bowyers, glaziers, plumbers, upholsterers, painters, slaters, sievewrights and coopers.—They have a double representation in the town-council; one deacon is chosen to represent the wrights, and another the masons.

The cordiners are better known by the name of shoemakers

With the waulkers the hatters are incorporated.

And the dyers with the bonnetmakers.

ELECTION of DEACONS.

IN order to form the council, it is neceſſary to begin with the election of deacons for each of theſe crafts.—On the third council-day (Wedneſday) preceding the feaſt of Michaelmas, yearly, the provoſt, bailies, and council for the year, confiſting of nineteen perſons only (excluding always the ſix council deacons), ſhall convene, and call before them the preſent fourteen deacons, every one ſeverally, and inquire their opinion and judgment of the beſt and worthieſt men of their reſpective crafts *; and the provoſt, bailies, and council ſhall then proceed to nominate and leet three of the moſt diſcreet and beſt qualified perſons for each craft (whereof the old deacon ſhall always be one), who are burgeſſes and freemen of the city, and who have been maſters of their crafts for two years

---

* This was according to the original ſet of King James VI. but the decreet arbitral of Archibald Duke of Argyle in 1730, regulates this matter as follows: " Ordains that the uſage and cuſtom of preſenting leets of ſix perſons made by the ſeveral incorporations, and atteſted by their reſpective clerks, to the magiſtrates and council, in order to their making ſhort leets of three for election of deacons, be inviolably for ever obſerved, and that the ſhort leets be returned by them out of the ſaid leets of ſix, regularly and legally made and atteſted."

at least. After which the fourteen leets shall be delivered to their respective deacons, and each deacon, on the day thereafter, shall convene his craft, and of the three persons in the leet, shall elect one to be deacon of that craft for the ensuing year:— And upon the next council day after the said election, the old deacons, attended by some of the masters of the crafts, shall present the new deacons to the council, who shall authorise them in their offices, and receive them in place of the old deacons.

ELECTION *of* COUNCIL DEACONS.

ON the said day of presenting the new deacons, the provost, bailies, and council, consisting of nineteen, shall chuse, from among the said fourteen deacons, six persons to sit in council for the ensuing year, and to be called council deacons; and the six deacons, who were formerly upon the council, shall be removed, and have no future vote in council, unless they be re-elected.

ELECTION *of* NEW COUNCIL, *and of Merchant and Trades Counsellors.*

UPON Wednesday next immediately preceding Michaelmas, yearly, the provost, bailies, dean of guild, and treasurer; the old provost, old bailies, old dean of guild, and old treasurer; three merchant counsellors, two trades counsellors, and six council deacons, in all twenty-five persons, and twenty six votes, (the provost always having two), shall convene and chuse a new council of eighteen for the ensuing year; and as the provost, bailies, dean of guild, and treasurer for the present year, and the six new council deacons, make thirteen persons thereof,—so they shall add and chuse three of the most respectable merchants of the city to be merchant counsellors, and likewise two reputable merchants of the city to be merchant counsellors, and likewise two reputable craftsmen to be trades counsellors, (in place of the five former counsellors); and these eighteen to be called the new council. And if any of the merchant counsellors so chosen be afterwards upon the leets for Magistrates, and be promoted thereto, another reputable merchant shall be chosen counsellor in his room on the day he is so promoted.

Fixing the Leets for MAGISTRATES.

ON the Friday next thereafter, the said new council of eighteen, and the old council of twelve, (viz. the old provost, old bailies, old dean of guild, and old treasurer, the three old merchant counsellors, and the two old trades counsellors) in all thirty persons, (and thirty one votes,) shall convene to fix the leets for magistrates for the ensuing year;

" and these thirty persons solemnly protesting before God that they shall chuse the persons most fit for these offices, without favour, hatred, or any kind of collusion," shall then begin and chuse for each of the seven magistrates a leet of three; that is, for the provost a leet of three, (the present provost being one of them); for each of the four bailies a leet of three; for the dean of guild a leet of three (including the present dean), and for the treasurer a leet of three (the present included) *. And a majority of votes of the said thirty persons to determine every name to be put in these leets.

ELECTION of MAGISTRATES.

ON Tuesday next after Michaelmas, yearly, there shall convene the said thirty persons of new and old council, and also the remaining eight of the fourteen deacons who are not of the council, (but are in this case extraordinary council deacons), in all thirty eight persons, and thirty nine votes; —and beginning at the leet for provost, " they shall all in their own ranks give their votes to such as they find meet for the good of the town, according

---

* The Duke of Argyle's decreet-arbitral contains the following clause:—" Finds that according to the set of the town, there must be three persons in every leet for the several offices of provost, dean of guild, and treasurer, and twelve persons in the leet for bailies: but it is not determined by the set whether the said leets should contain one and twenty different persons; and the usage appears to be in the contrary, which therefore ought to prevail."

to their confcience and knowledge, without fee or favour;' and on whom the greateft number of votes fhall fall, he fhall be fworn, received, and admitted provoft for that year enfuing;—and fo proceed, in the fame manner, through the leets for the bailies, dean of guild, and treafurer, till the faid election be completely ended.

AND the election being juftly and duly declared and minuted in the council books, the faid newly elected provoft; bailies, dean of guild, and treafurer, being added to the eighteen council formerly elected, and making in all twenty five perfons,—they only (and no others) fhall have the full government and adminiftration of the hail commonweal of the city, in all things, for one year enfuing:

EXCEPTING always the cafes following, in which the whole fourteen deacons of crafts fhall be called to give their fpecial vote and confultation, viz. an election of the provoft, bailies, dean of guild, and treafurer (as above); an election for a member of parliament; in fetting of feus, or any manner of tacks (except the yearly rouping of the town's good on Martinmas even); in giving of benefices or other offices in the burgh; in granting of extents, contributions, and ficklike; building of common works; and in difpofing of the common good of the fum of twenty pounds together.

AND if any one more of the eight extraordinary deacons, being perfonally warned to a meeting for any of the above purpofes, and abfent himfelf, then the laft deacon who preceded him, or any other who was in the leet with him at the laft election, fhall fupply his place for the time; and he alfo being abfent (though perfonally warned),— then the meeting are empowered to proceed to bufinefs without them.

THAT no perfon whatever be chofen provoft, bailie, dean of guild, or treafurer, although they be burgeffes of the city, unlefs they have been one year at leaft in the council before.— That no perfon be upon the council above two years together, unlefs he be chofen into office, fuch as provoft, bailie, dean of guild, or treafurer; in that cafe he is *ex officio*, a counfellor.— That no deacon of a craft fhall be continued in his faid office of deacon above two years together.

That the provoft, dean of guild, and treafurer, fhall not be elected or continued in their offices longer than one, or, at moft, two years together at a time: And the bailies fhall only be one year bailie, one year old bailie, and one year free of office, and fhall not be put in leets for bailies till thofe years be paft. That whoever has ferved the office of Dean of Guild fhall be capable, *at any time afterwards*, to be chosen provost or bailie, as the council shall think fit: And the treasurer shall also be capable to be chosen bailie, but not till his accounts, as treasurer, are finally fitted and approved by the council.

THAT the right of calling the council, ordinary and extraordinary, belongs to the provost or preses of the meeting; and upon an execution returned to the members being summoned by the said provost or preses his order, thirteen of the ordinary, and seventeen of the extraordinary council, may proceed and act in the same manner as if all the members were present; but if the provost or preses shall happen to neglect, or shall refuse to call a council on Wednesday (the ordinary council day), a majority of the said council may, forty eight hours preceding the ordinary and stated time of meeting, require the aforesaid provost or preses, under form of instrument, to call a council, and upon his refusal or neglect to comply with the demand so made, the majority of the said council may meet on the said usual and stated time, and proceed to do business.

THAT the provost has right to the first vote in every matter and thing, and to a calling vote in case of an equality, and to no other or further vote in any case whatever.

THAT the deacons extraordinary, or not of the council, have a vote in chufing proxies for the abfent members of the ordinary council at the annual election, in all fteps where they have a right to be prefent.

THAT the faid extraordinary deacons of crafts have right to give their fpecial vote and confultation, annually, in electing and chufing the members of the dean of guild court of Edinburgh; but that they have no vote in the election of the officers of the train bands, the conftables, and bailies of the public markets of the city, and their affiftants, kirk and college treafurers, ftent-mafters, and auditors of the town's accounts; nor in electing and chufing the baron bailies of the fuburbs, namely, the bailies of Leith, Canongate, Portfburgh, and Caltoun; the magiftrates and ordinary council having the only right of chufing the faid officers.

THAT no perfon who has deferted and given over the practice and exercife of his trade and occupation within the city of Edinburgh and liberties thereof, unlefs he refide within the faid town or liberties, and at the fame time fubject himfelf to the common burdens of the town and incorporation whereof he is free, or who is received as a member or fervant in any of the town's hofpitals, or who is a penfioner of the town or trade, or has or enjoys any benefit or incrative office from the town or trade, or, who, at any time within fix months preceding, has been received, or was member, fervant, or penfioner as aforefaid, or held or enjoyed fuch benefice or incrative office hath, or ought to have any vote in the election of a deacon, or other officer of the incorporation, or in making up leets in order to the election of a deacon or other officer, or to act or vote in any meeting whatfoever, of any incorporation within the faid city.

THAT the expence of all public treats ought to be previoufly authorifed by the council, and attefted when laid out by two of the council, or more, who are hereby ordained to write, or caufe to be written on the bills. the date and occafion of the expence, and the perfon's name to whom the fame was paid, or is due; and to fign the faid bills and report, and produce them in council within a month at fartheft after the faid expence is incurred.

THAT neither the merchants among themfelves, nor the crafts and their deacons among themfelves, fhall make any particular or general conventions, as merchants with merchants, deacons with deacons, deacons with crafts, or crafts among themfelves, without the advice and confent of the provoft, bailies, and council.

EXCEPTING always, that the dean of guild may assemble his brethren and council in their guild courts, conform to the antient laws and privileges of the guildry: And any craft may convene together among themselves, for the chusing of their deacons at the time appointed thereto, and in manner before expressed; making of masters, and trying of their handy work, allenarly: And if any brethren, or deacons of crafts, shall find out, or devise any good heads that may tend to the good of their craft, they shall propone the same to the magistrates, who shall set forward an act or statute thereupon.

THAT the council, ordinary and extraordinary, have the sole power and right of governing the Trinity Hospital, and cannot delegate the same to any other person or persons whatsoever.

THAT the accompts of the town be fitted and audited within the year to which the said accompts relate, or within three months after the expiration of the said year; and that no article of debursement of the town's money ought to be allowed unless the same be sufficiently vouched.

F I N I S.

www.ingramcontent.com/pod-product-compliance
Lightning Source LLC
Chambersburg PA
CBHW031454160426
4319SCB00010BB/970